THE FIFTH
RISK

MICHAEL LEWIS

THE FIFTH RISK

W. W. NORTON & COMPANY

Independent Publishers Since 1923

New York | London

For information about permission to reproduce selections from this book,
write to Permissions, W. W. Norton & Company, Inc.,
500 Fifth Avenue, New York, NY 10110

For information about special discounts for bulk purchases, please contact
W. W. Norton Special Sales at specialsales@wwnorton.com or 800-233-4830

Manufacturing by LSC Communications Harrisonburg
Book design by Chris Welch Design
Production manager: Julia Druskin
Digital production: Joe Lops

Library of Congress Cataloging-in-Publication Data

Names: Lewis, Michael (Michael M.), author.
Title: The fifth risk / Michael Lewis.
Description: First edition. | New York : W. W. Norton & Company, 2018.
Identifiers: LCCN 2018038204 | ISBN 9781324002642 (hardcover)
Subjects: LCSH: United States—Politics and government—2017– |
Administrative agencies—United States—Management. | Government
executives—United States. | Public administration—United States. |
Civil service—United States.
Classification: LCC E912 .L48 2018 | DDC 320.973/090512—dc23
LC record available at https://lccn.loc.gov/2018038204

W. W. Norton & Company, Inc., 500 Fifth Avenue, New York, N.Y. 10110
www.wwnorton.com

W. W. Norton & Company Ltd., 15 Carlisle Street, London W1D 3BS

1 2 3 4 5 6 7 8 9 0

for
Tom Wolfe
In Memoriam

Donald J. Trump ✔
@realDonaldTrump

Very organized process taking place as I decide on Cabinet and many other positions. I am the only one who knows who the finalists are!

9:55 PM - 15 Nov 2016

25,572 Retweets   **112,055** Likes

CONTENTS

THE FIFTH RISK

LOST IN TRANSITION

CHRIS CHRISTIE NOTICED a piece in the *New York Times*—that's how it all started. The New Jersey governor had dropped out of the presidential race in February 2016 and thrown what support he had behind Donald Trump. In late April he saw the article. It described meetings between representatives of the remaining candidates still in the race—Trump, John Kasich, Ted Cruz, Hillary Clinton, and Bernie Sanders—and the Obama White House. Anyone who still had any kind of shot at becoming president of the United States apparently needed to start preparing to run the federal government. The guy Trump sent to the meeting was, in Christie's estimation, comically underqualified. Christie called up Trump's campaign manager, Corey Lewandowski, to ask why this critical job hadn't been handed to someone who actually knew something about government. "We don't have anyone," said Lewandowski.

Christie volunteered himself for the job: head of the Donald Trump presidential transition team. "It's the next best thing to being president," he told friends. "You get to plan the presidency." He went to see Trump about it. Trump said he didn't want a presidential transition team. Why did anyone need to plan *anything* before he actually became president? *It's legally required*, said Christie. Trump asked where the money was going to come from to pay for the transition team. Christie explained that Trump could either pay for it himself or take it out of campaign funds. Trump didn't want to pay for it himself. He didn't want to take it out of campaign funds, either, but he agreed, grudgingly, that Christie should go ahead and raise a separate fund to pay for his transition team. "But not too much!" he said.

And so Christie set out to prepare for the unlikely event that Donald Trump would one day be elected president of the United States. Not everyone in Trump's campaign was happy to see him on the job. In June, Christie received a call from Trump adviser Paul Manafort. "The kid is paranoid about you," Manafort said. The kid was Jared Kushner, Trump's son-in-law. Back in 2005, when he was U.S. attorney for the District of New Jersey, Christie had prosecuted and jailed Kushner's father, Charles, for tax fraud. Christie's investigation revealed, in the bargain, that Charles Kushner had hired a prostitute to seduce his own brother-in-law, whom he suspected of cooperating with Christie, videotaped the sexual encounter, and sent the tape to his sister. The Kushners apparently took their grudges seriously, and Christie sensed that Jared still harbored one against him. On the other hand, Trump, whom Christie considered almost a friend, couldn't have cared less. He'd invited Christie to his and Melania's wedding and then pressed him to attend his daughter, Ivanka, and Jared Kushner's wedding. *That'd be awkward!* said Christie. *I'm paying for the wedding and I don't give a shit*, said Donald.

Christie viewed Jared as one of those people who thinks that, because he's rich, he must also be smart. Still, he had a certain cunning about him. And Christie soon found himself reporting everything he did to prepare for a Trump administration to an "executive committee." The committee consisted of Jared, Ivanka Trump, Donald Trump Jr., Eric Trump, Paul Manafort, Steve Mnuchin, and Jeff Sessions. "I'm kind of like the church elder who double-counts the collection plate every Sunday for the pastor," said Sessions, who appeared uncomfortable with the entire situation. The elder's job became more complicated in July 2016, when Trump was formally named the Republican nominee. The transition team now moved into an office in downtown Washington, DC, and went looking for people to occupy the top five hundred jobs in the federal government. They needed to fill all the cabinet positions, of course, but also a whole bunch of others that no one in the Trump campaign even knew existed. It's not obvious how you find the next secretary of state, much less the next secretary of transportation—never mind who should sit on the board of trustees of the Barry Goldwater Scholarship and Excellence in Education Foundation.

By August, 130 people were showing up every day, and hundreds more working part-time, at Trump transition headquarters, on the corner of Seventeenth Street and Pennsylvania Avenue. The transition team made lists of likely candidates for all five hundred jobs, plus other lists of informed people to roll into the various federal agencies the day after the election, to be briefed on whatever the federal agencies were doing. They gathered the names for these lists by traveling the country and talking to people: Republicans who had served in government, Trump's closest advisers, recent occupants of the jobs that needed filling. Then they set about investigating any candidates for glaring flaws and embarrassing secrets and conflicts of interest. At the end of each week Christie handed over binders, with lists of names of people who might do the jobs well, to Jared and Donald and Eric and the others. "They probed everything," says a senior Trump transition official. "'Who is this person?' 'Where did this person come from?' They only ever rejected one person, Paul Manafort's secretary."

The first time Donald Trump paid attention to any of this was when he read about it in the newspaper. The story revealed that Trump's very own transition team, led by New Jersey governor Chris Christie, had raised several million dollars to pay the staff. The moment he saw it, Trump called Steve Bannon, the chief executive of his campaign, from his office, on the twenty-sixth floor of Trump Tower, and told him to come immediately to his residence, many floors above. Bannon stepped off the elevator to find the governor of New Jersey seated on a sofa, being hollered at. Trump was apoplectic, actually yelling, *You're stealing my money! You're stealing my fucking money! What the fuck is this??* Seeing Bannon, Trump turned on *him* and screamed, *Why are you letting him steal my fucking money?* Bannon and Christie together set out to explain to Trump federal law. Months before the election, the law said, the nominees of the two major parties were expected to prepare to take control of the government. The government supplied them with office space in downtown Washington, DC, along with computers and trash cans and so on, but the campaigns paid their people. To which Trump replied, *Fuck the law. I don't give a fuck about the law. I want my fucking money.* Bannon and Christie tried to explain that Trump couldn't have both his money and a transition.

Shut it down, said Trump. Shut down the transition.

Here Christie and Bannon parted ways. Neither thought it was a good idea to shut down the transition, but each had his own misgivings. Christie thought that Trump had little chance of running the government without a formal transition. Bannon wasn't so sure if Trump would ever get his mind around running the federal government: he just thought it would look bad if Trump didn't at least seem to prepare. Seeing that Trump wasn't listening to Christie, he said, "What do you think *Morning Joe* will say—if you shut down your transition?" What *Morning Joe* would say—or at least what Bannon thought it would say—was that Trump was closing his presidential transition office because he didn't think he had any chance of being president.

Trump stopped hollering. For the first time he seemed actually to have listened.

"That makes sense," he said.

With that, Christie went back to preparing for a Trump administration. He tried to stay out of the news, but that proved difficult. From time to time Trump would see something in the paper about Christie's fund-raising and become upset all over again. The money people donated to his campaign Trump considered, effectively, his own. He thought the planning and forethought pointless. At one point he turned to Christie and said, "Chris, you and I are so smart that we can leave the victory party two hours early and do the transition ourselves."

At that moment in American history, if you could somehow organize the entire population into a single line, all three hundred fifty million people, ordered not by height or weight or age but by each citizen's interest in the federal government, and Donald Trump loitered somewhere near one end of it, Max Stier would occupy the other.

By the fall of 2016 Max Stier might have been the American with the greatest understanding of how the U.S. government actually worked. Oddly, for an American of his age and status, he'd romanticized public service since he was a child. He'd gone through Yale in the mid-1980s and Stanford Law School in the early 1990s without ever being tempted by money or anything else. He thought the U.S. government was the single most important and most interesting institution in the history of the planet and couldn't imagine doing anything but working to improve it. A few years out of law school he'd met a financier named Sam Heyman, who was as disturbed as Max was by how uninterested talented young people were in government work. Max persuaded Heyman to set aside $25 million for him so that he might create an organization to address the problem.

Max soon realized that to attract talented young people to government service he'd need to turn the government into a place talented young people wanted to work. He'd need to *fix* the United States government. Partnership for Public Service, as Max called his organization, was not nearly as dull as its name. It trained civil servants to be business managers; it brokered new relationships across the federal government; it surveyed the federal workforce to identify specific management failures and success; and it lobbied Congress to fix deep structural problems. It was Max Stier who had persuaded Congress to pass the laws that made it so annoyingly difficult for Donald Trump to avoid preparing to be president.

Anyway, from the point of view of a smart, talented person trying to decide whether to work for the U.S. government, the single most glaring defect was the absence of an upside. The jobs weren't well paid compared to their equivalents in the private sector. And the only time government employees were recognized was if they screwed up—in which case they often became the wrong kind of famous. In 2002 Max created an annual black tie, Oscarslike awards ceremony to celebrate people who had done extraordinary things in government. Every year the Sammies—as Max called them, in honor of his original patron—attracted a few more celebrities and a bit more media attention. And every year the list of achievements was mind-blowing. A guy in the Energy Department (Frazer Lockhart) organized the first successful cleanup of a nuclear weapons factory, in Rocky Flats, Colorado, and had brought it in sixty years early and $30 billion under budget. A woman at the Federal Trade Commission (Eileen Harrington) had built the Do Not Call Registry, which spared the entire country from trillions of irritating sales pitches. A National Institutes of Health researcher (Steven Rosenberg) had pioneered immunotherapy, which had successfully treated previously incurable cancers. There were hundreds of fantastically important success stories in the United States government. They just never got told.

Max knew an astonishing number of them. He'd detected a pattern: a surprising number of the people responsible for them were first-generation Americans who had come from places without well-functioning governments. People who had lived without government were more likely to find meaning in it. On the other hand, people who had never experienced a collapsed state were slow to appreciate a state that had not yet collapsed. That was maybe Max's biggest challenge: explaining the value of this enterprise at the center of a democratic society to people who either took it for granted or imagined it as a pernicious force in their lives over which they had no control. He'd explain that the federal government provided services that the private sector couldn't or wouldn't: medical care for veterans, air traffic control, national highways, food safety guidelines. He'd explain that the federal government was an engine of opportunity: millions of American children, for instance, would have found it even harder than they did to make the most of their lives without the basic nutrition supplied by the federal government. When all else failed, he'd explain the many places the U.S. government stood between Americans and the things that might kill them. "The basic role of government is to keep us safe," he'd say.

The United States government employed two million people, 70 percent of them one way or another in national security. It managed a portfolio of risks that no private person, or corporation, was able to manage. Some of the risks were easy to imagine: a financial crisis, a hurricane, a terrorist attack. Most weren't: the risk, say, that some prescription drug proves to be both so addictive and so accessible that each year it kills more Americans than were killed in action by the peak of the Vietnam War. Many of the risks that fell into the government's lap felt so remote as to be unreal: that a cyberattack left half the country without electricity, or that some airborne virus wiped out millions, or that economic inequality reached the point where it triggered a violent revolution. Maybe the least visible risks were of things *not* happening that, with better government, might have happened. A cure for cancer, for instance.

Enter the presidential transition. A bad transition took

this entire portfolio of catastrophic risks—the biggest portfolio of such risks ever managed by a single institution in the history of the world—and made all the bad things more likely to happen and the good things less likely to happen. Even before Max created an organization to fix the federal government, the haphazard nature of presidential transitions drove him nuts. "We have a legacy government that hasn't kept up with the world we live in, largely because of disruptions from bad transitions," he said. "People don't understand that a bungled transition becomes a bungled presidency." The new people taking over the job of running the government were at best only partially informed, and often deeply suspicious of whatever happened to be going on before they arrived. By the time they fully grasped the problems they were dealing with, it was time to go. "It's *Groundhog Day*," said Max. "The new people come in and think that the previous administration and the civil service are lazy or stupid. Then they actually get to know the place they are managing. And when they leave they say, 'This was a really hard job, and those are the best people I've ever worked with.' This happens over and over and over."

Most of the big problems inside the U.S. government were of the practical management sort and had nothing to do with political ideology. A mundane but important example was how hard it was for any government agency to hire new people. Some agencies couldn't hire anyone without sixty different people signing off on him. The George W. Bush administration had begun to attack that particular mundane problem. The Obama administration, instead of running with the work done during the Bush years, had simply started all over again.

Max Stier's Partnership for Public Service had helped to push through three separate laws related to the transition. In 2010 Congress gave free office space and other resources to the nominees of the two major political parties right after the summer conventions. "The reason campaigns didn't prepare is that they thought it would cost them politically: no one wanted to be seen measuring the drapes," said Max. "The idea was to give the nominees of the major political parties cover to do what they should do." In 2011–2012, to enable the president to put people in jobs more quickly, Congress reduced the number of presidential appointments that required Senate confirmation from about 1,400 to roughly 1,200—still over a thousand too many, in Max's view, but a start. Finally, in 2015, Congress required the sitting president to prepare in various ways to hand the government over to his or her successor. The person who had already taken the test was now required by law to help the person who may not have studied for it.

As the 2016 presidential election approached, Max was about as hopeful as he'd ever been that the United States government would be handed from one leader to another with minimum stupidity. His partnership had worked with both the Clinton and the Trump campaigns. "Their work was good," said Max. He was disappointed with Barack Obama in some ways. President Obama had been slow to engage with the federal workforce. He'd appointed some poor managers to run some agencies. The fiasco of the rollout of HealthCare.gov was not an accident but a by-product of bad management. But Obama's preparations to hand over the government had been superb: the Obama administration had created what amounted to the best course ever on the inner workings of the most powerful institution on earth. What could go wrong?

———

Chris Christie was sitting on a sofa beside Donald Trump when Pennsylvania was finally called. It was one thirty-five in the morning, but that wasn't the only reason the feeling in the room was odd. Mike Pence went to kiss his wife, Karen, and she turned away from him. "You got what you wanted, Mike," she said, "now leave me alone." She wouldn't so much as say hello to Trump. Trump himself just stared at the tube without saying anything, like a man with a pair of twos whose bluff has been called. His campaign hadn't even bothered to prepare an acceptance speech. It wasn't hard to see why Trump hadn't seen the point in preparing to take over the federal government: Why study for a test you'll never need to take? Why take the risk of discovering you might at your very best be a C student? This was the real part of becoming president of the United States. And, Christie thought, it scared the crap out of the president-elect.

Not long after the people on TV announced that Trump had won Pennsylvania, Jared Kushner grabbed Christie anxiously and said, "We have to have a transition meeting tomorrow morning!" Even before that meeting, Christie had made sure that Trump knew the protocol for his discussions with foreign leaders. The transition team had prepared a document to let him know how these were meant to go. The first few calls were easy—the very first was always with the prime minister of Great Britain— but two dozen calls in you were talking to some klepto- crat and tiptoeing around sensitive security issues. Before any of the calls could be made, however, the president of Egypt called in to the switchboard at Trump Tower and somehow got the operator to put him straight through to Trump. "Trump was like . . . *I love the Bangles! You know that song 'Walk Like an Egyptian'?*" recalled one of his advis- ers on the scene.

That had been the first hint Christie had of trouble. He'd asked Jared Kushner what that was about, and Jared had simply said, *Donald ran a very unconventional campaign, and he's not going to follow any of the protocols.* The next hint that the transition might not go as planned came from Mike Pence. Now, incredibly, *Vice President-elect Mike Pence.* Christie met with Pence the day after the election, to discuss the previous lists of people who had been vetted for jobs. The meeting began with a prayer, followed by Pence's first, ominous question: Why isn't Puzder on the list for Labor? Andrew Puzder, the head of CKE Restau- rants, the holding company for Hardee's and Carl's Jr., wanted to be the secretary of labor. Christie explained that Puzder's ex-wife had accused him of abuse, and his fast-food restaurant employees had complained of mistreatment. Even if he was somehow the ideal candidate to become the next secretary of labor, he wouldn't survive his Senate confirmation hearings. (Trump ignored the advice and nominated Puzder. In the controversy that followed, Puzder not only failed to be confirmed but stepped down from his job at the fast-food company.)

After meeting with Pence, Christie was scheduled to brief the Trump children and Jared and the other members of Trump's inner circle. He was surprised to find, suddenly included in this group, retired army lieutenant general Michael Flynn. Flynn was a job seeker the transition team had found reasons to be extremely wary of. Now he wanted to be named Trump's national security adviser, which was maybe the most important job in the entire national security apparatus. The national security team inside the Trump transition—staffed with senior former military and intelligence officials—had thought that an especially bad idea. Flynn's name wasn't on the list. But here he was, in the meeting to decide who would do what in the Trump administration, and Ivanka was asking him which job he'd like to have.

Before Christie could intercede, Steve Bannon grabbed him and asked to see him privately. Christie followed Bannon to his office impatiently. *Hey, this is going to have to be quick*, said Christie.

It's really quick, said Bannon. *You're out.*

Why? asked Christie, stunned.

We're making a change.

Okay, what are we changing?
You.
Why?
It's really not important.

The method of his execution was unsurprising: Trump always avoided firing people himself. The man who played Mr. You're Fired on TV avoided personal confrontation in real life. The surprise was that it was being done now, just when the work of the transition team was most critical. Only when Christie threatened to go down and tell reporters that Steve Bannon had fired him did Bannon concede, "It was Jared."

In the days after the election, the people in the building on Seventeenth and Pennsylvania were meant to move to another building in downtown Washington, a kind of White House-in-waiting. They soon discovered that the lists that they had created of people to staff the Trump administration were not the lists that mattered. There was now this other list, of people allowed into the new building, and most of their names weren't on it. "People would show up to the new building and say, 'Let me in,' and the Secret Service would say, 'Sorry, you're not on the list,'" said a civil servant who worked in the new building. It wasn't just Chris Christie who'd been fired. It was the entire transition team—though no one ever told them so directly. As Nancy Cook later reported in *Politico*, Bannon visited the transition headquarters a few days after he'd given Christie the news, and made a show of tossing the work the people there had done for Donald Trump into the garbage can. Trump was going to handle the transition more or less by himself. Not even Steve Bannon thought this was a good idea. "I was fucking nervous as shit," Bannon later told friends. "I go, 'Holy fuck, this guy [Trump] doesn't know anything. And he doesn't give a shit.'"

I

TAIL RISK

O N THE MORNING after the election, November 9, 2016, the people who ran the U.S. Department of Energy turned up in their offices and waited. They had cleared thirty desks and freed up thirty parking spaces. They didn't know exactly how many people they'd host that day, but whoever won the election would surely be sending a small army into the Department of Energy, and to every other federal agency. The morning after he was elected president, eight years earlier, Barack Obama had sent between thirty and forty people into the Department of Energy. The Department of Energy staff planned to deliver to Trump's people the same talks, from the same five-inch-thick three-ring binders with the Department of Energy seal on them, that they would have given to the Clinton people. "Nothing had to be changed," said one former Department of Energy staffer. "They'd be done always with the intention that, either party wins, nothing changes."

By afternoon the silence was deafening. "Day 1, we're ready to go," says a former senior White House official. "Day 2 it was, 'Maybe they'll call us?'"

"Teams were going around, 'Have you heard from them?'" recalls another staffer who had prepared for the transition. "'Have you gotten anything? I haven't got anything.'"

"The election happened," remembers Elizabeth Sherwood-Randall, then deputy secretary of the DOE. "And he won. And then there was radio silence. We were prepared for *the next day*. And nothing happened." Across the federal government the Trump people weren't anywhere to be found. The few places they did turn up, they appeared confused and unprepared. A small group attended a briefing at the State Department, for instance, only to learn that the briefings they needed to hear were classified. None of the Trump people had security clearance—or, for that matter, any experience in foreign policy—and so they weren't allowed to receive an education. On his visits to the White House soon after the election, Jared Kushner expressed surprise that so much of its staff seemed to be leaving. "It was like he thought it was a corporate acquisition or something," says an Obama White House staffer. "He thought everyone just stayed."

Even in normal times the people who take over the United States government can be surprisingly ignorant about it. As a longtime career civil servant in the Department of Energy who has watched four different administrations show up to try to run the place put it, "You always have the issue of maybe they don't understand what the department does." To address that problem, a year before he left office, Barack Obama had instructed a lot of knowledgeable people across his administration, including fifty or so inside the DOE, to gather the knowledge that his successor would need in order to understand the government he or she was taking charge of. The Bush administration had done the same for Obama, and Obama had been grateful for their efforts. He told his staff that their goal should be to ensure an even smoother transfer of power than the Bush people had achieved.

That had proved to be a huge undertaking. Thousands of people inside the federal government had spent the better part of a year drawing a vivid picture of it for the benefit of the new administration. The United States government might be the most complicated organization on the face of the earth. Its two million federal employees take orders from four thousand political appointees. Dysfunction is baked into the structure of the thing: the subordinates know that their bosses will be replaced every four or eight years, and that the direction of their enterprises might change overnight—with an election or a war or some other political event. Still, many of the problems our government grapples with aren't particularly ideological, and the Obama people tried to keep their political ideology out of the briefings. "You don't have to agree with our politics," as the former senior White House official put it. "You just have to understand how we got here. Zika, for instance. You might disagree with how we approached it. You don't have to agree. You just have to understand why we approached it that way."

How to stop a virus, how to take a census, how to determine if some foreign country is seeking to obtain a nuclear weapon or if North Korean missiles can reach Kansas City: these are enduring technical problems. The people appointed by a newly elected president to solve these problems have roughly seventy-five days to learn from their predecessors. After the inauguration, a lot of deeply knowledgeable people will scatter to the four winds and be forbidden, by federal law, from initiating any contact with their replacements. The period between the election and the inauguration has the feel of an AP chemistry class to which half the students have turned up late and are forced to scramble to grab the notes taken by the other half, before the final.

Two weeks after the election, the Obama people inside the DOE read in the newspapers that Trump had created a small "Landing Team." It was led by, and mostly consisted of, a man named Thomas Pyle, president of the American Energy Alliance, which, upon inspection, proved to be a Washington, DC, propaganda machine funded with millions of dollars from ExxonMobil and Koch Industries. Pyle himself had served as a Koch Industries lobbyist and ran a business on the side writing editorials attacking the DOE's attempts to reduce the dependence of the American economy on carbon. Pyle said that his role on the Landing Team was "voluntary" and added that he could not disclose who appointed him, due to a confidentiality agreement. The people running the DOE were by then seriously alarmed. "We first learned of Pyle's appointment

on the Monday of Thanksgiving week," recalls Kevin
Knobloch, then DOE chief of staff. "We sent word to him
that the secretary and his deputy would meet with him as
soon as possible. He said he would like that but could not
do it until after Thanksgiving."

A month after the election, Pyle arrived for a meeting with Energy Secretary Ernest Moniz, Deputy Secretary Sherwood-Randall, and Knobloch. Moniz, a nuclear
physicist who was then on leave from MIT and who had
served as deputy secretary during the Clinton administration, is widely viewed, even by many Republicans, as
understanding and loving the DOE better than any person
on earth. Pyle appeared to have no interest in anything he
had to say. "He did not seem motivated to spend a lot of
time understanding the place," says Sherwood-Randall.
"He didn't bring a pencil or a piece of paper. He didn't
ask questions. He spent an hour. That was it. He never
asked to meet with us again." Afterward, Knobloch says,
he suggested that Pyle visit one day each week until the
inauguration, and that Pyle agreed to do it—but then he
never showed up. "It's a head-scratcher," says Knobloch.
"It's a thirty-billion-dollar-a-year organization with about
a hundred ten thousand employees. Industrial sites across
the country. Very serious stuff. If you're going to run it,
why wouldn't you want to know something about it?"

There was a reason Obama had appointed nuclear physicists to run the place: it, like the problems it grappled with,
was technical and complicated. Moniz had helped lead
the U.S. negotiations with Iran precisely because he knew

which parts of their nuclear energy program they must surrender if they were to be prevented from obtaining a nuclear weapon. For a decade before Knobloch joined the DOE, in June 2013, he had served as president of the Union of Concerned Scientists. "I had worked closely with DOE throughout my career," he says. "I thought I knew and understood the agency. But when I came in I thought, Holy cow."

Deputy Secretary Elizabeth Sherwood-Randall has spent her thirty-year career working on reducing the world's supply of weapons of mass destruction—she led the U.S. mission to remove chemical weapons from Syria. But like everyone else who came to work at the DOE, she'd grown accustomed to no one knowing what the department actually did. When she'd called home, back in 2013, to tell them that President Obama had nominated her to be second-in-command of the place, her mother said, "Well, darling, I have no idea what the Department of Energy does, but you've always had a lot of energy, so I'm sure you'll be perfect for the role."

The Trump administration had no clearer idea what she did with her day than her mother. And yet, according to Sherwood-Randall, they were certain they didn't need to hear anything she had to say before they took over her job. Pyle eventually sent over a list of seventy-four questions he wanted answers to. His list addressed some of the subjects covered in the briefing materials, but also a few not:

Can you provide a list of all Department of Energy employees or contractors who have attended any

Interagency Working Group on the Social Cost of Carbon meetings?

Can you provide a list of Department employees or contractors who attended any of the Conference of the Parties (under the United Nations Framework Convention on Climate Change) in the last five years?

That, in a nutshell, was the spirit of the Trump enterprise. "It reminded me of McCarthyism," says Sherwood-Randall.

It says a great deal about the mind-set of career civil servants that the DOE employee in charge of overseeing the transition set out to answer even the most offensive questions. Her attitude, like the attitude of the permanent staff, was, *We are meant to serve our elected masters, however odious they might be.* "When the questions got leaked to the press, she was really upset," says the former DOE staffer. The only reason that the DOE did not serve up the names of people who had educated themselves about climate change, and thus exposed themselves to the wrath of the new administration, was that the old administration was still in charge: "We aren't answering these questions," Secretary Moniz had said simply.

After Pyle's list of questions wound up on Bloomberg News, the Trump administration disavowed them, but a signal had been sent: *We don't want you to help us understand; we want to find out who you are and punish you.* Pyle vanished from the scene. According to a former Obama official, he was replaced by a handful of young ideologues who called themselves "the Beachhead Team." "They mainly ran around the building insulting people," says a former Obama official. "There was a mentality that everything that government does is stupid and bad and the people in it are stupid and bad," says another. They demanded to know the names and salaries of the twenty highest-paid people in the national science labs overseen by the DOE. They'd eventually delete the contact list with the email addresses of all DOE-funded scientists—apparently to make it more difficult for them to communicate with one another. "These people were insane," says the former DOE staffer. "They weren't prepared. They didn't know what they were doing."

"We had tried desperately to prepare them," said Tarak Shah, chief of staff for the DOE's $6 billion basic-science program. "But that required them to show up. And bring qualified people. But they didn't. They didn't ask for even an introductory briefing. Like, 'What do you do?'" The Obama people did what they could to preserve the institution's understanding of itself. "We were prepared for them to start wiping out documents," said Shah. "So we prepared a public website to transfer the stuff onto it—if needed."

The one concrete action the Trump transition team took before Inauguration Day was to attempt to clear the DOE and other federal agencies of people appointed by Obama. But there was actually a long history of even the appointees of one administration hanging around to help the new appointees of the next. The man who had served as the Department of Energy's chief financial officer during the Bush administration, for instance, stayed a year and a half into the Obama administration—simply because he had a detailed understanding of the money end of things that was hard to replicate quickly. The CFO of the department at the end of the Obama administration was a mild-mannered civil-servant type named Joe Hezir. He had no particular political identity and was widely thought to have done a good job—and so he half-expected a call from the Trump people asking him to stay on, just to keep the money side of things running smoothly. The call never came. No one even let him know his services were no longer required. Not knowing what else to do, but without anyone to replace him, the CFO of a $30 billion operation just up and left.

This was a loss. A lunch or two with the chief financial officer might have alerted the new administration to some of the terrifying risks they were leaving essentially unmanaged. Roughly half of the DOE's annual $30 billion budget is spent on maintaining and guarding our nuclear arsenal. Two billion of that goes to hunting down weapons-grade plutonium and uranium at loose in the world so that it doesn't fall into the hands of terrorists. In eight years alone—2010–2018—the DOE's National Nuclear Security Administration collected enough material to make 160 nuclear bombs. The department trains every international atomic-energy inspector; if nuclear power plants around the world are not producing weapons-grade material on the sly by reprocessing spent fuel rods and recovering plutonium, it's because of these people. The DOE also supplies radiation-detection equipment to enable other countries to detect bomb material making its way across national borders. To maintain the U.S. nuclear arsenal, it conducts endless expensive experiments on tiny amounts of nuclear material to try to understand what is happening to plutonium when it fissions, which, amazingly, no one really does. To study the process, it is funding what promises to be the next generation of supercomputers, which will in turn lead God knows where.

The Trump people didn't seem to grasp how much more than just energy the Department of Energy was about. They weren't totally oblivious to the nuclear arsenal, but even the nuclear arsenal didn't provoke in them much curiosity. "They were just looking for dirt, basically," said one of the people who briefed the Beachhead Team on national security issues. "'What is the Obama administration not letting you do to keep the country safe?'" The briefers were at pains to explain an especially sensitive aspect of national security: the United States no longer tests its nuclear weapons. Instead, it relies on physicists at three of the national labs—Los Alamos, Livermore, and Sandia—to simulate explosions, using old and decaying nuclear materials.

This is not a trivial exercise, and to do it we rely entirely on scientists who go to work at the national labs because the national labs are exciting places to work. They then wind up getting interested in the weapons program. That is, because maintaining the nuclear arsenal was just a by-product of the world's biggest science project, which also did things like investigating the origins of the universe. "Our weapons scientists didn't start out as weapons scientists," says Madelyn Creedon, who was second-in-command of the nuclear-weapons wing of the DOE, and who briefed the incoming administration, briefly. "They didn't understand that. The one question they asked was, 'Wouldn't you want the guy who grew up wanting to be a weapons scientist?' Well, actually, no. You wouldn't."

In the run-up to the Trump inauguration, the man inside the DOE in charge of the nuclear-weapons program—Frank Klotz was his name—was required to submit his resignation, as were the department's 137 other political appointees. Frank Klotz was a retired three-star air force lieutenant general with a PhD in politics from Oxford. The keeper of the nation's nuclear secrets had boxed up most of his books and memorabilia just like everyone else and was on his way out before anyone had apparently given the first thought to who might replace him. It was only after Secretary Moniz called U.S. senators to alert them to the disturbing vacancy, and the senators phoned Trump Tower sounding alarmed, that the Trump people called General Klotz and—on the *day before* Donald Trump was inaugurated as the forty-fifth president of the United States—asked him to bring back the stuff he had taken home and move back into his office. Aside from him, the people with the most intimate knowledge of the problems and the possibilities of the DOE walked out the door.

It was early June 2017 when I walked through the same

door to see what was going on. The DOE makes its home in a long rectangular cinder-block-like building propped up on concrete stilts, just off the National Mall. It's a jarring sight—as if someone had punched out a skyscraper and it never got back on its feet. It's relentlessly ugly in the way the swamps around Newark Airport are ugly—so ugly that its ugliness bends back around into a sneaky kind of beauty: it will make an excellent ruin. Inside, the place feels like a lab experiment to determine just how little aesthetic stimulation human beings can endure. The endless hallways are floored with white linoleum and almost insistently devoid of personality. "Like a hospital, without the stretchers," as one employee put it. But this place is at once desolate and urgent. People still work here, doing stuff that, if left undone, might result in unimaginable death and destruction.

By the time I arrived in Washington, the first eighth of Trump's first term was nearly complete, and his administration was still largely missing. He hadn't nominated anyone to serve as head of the Patent Office, for instance, or to run the Federal Emergency Management Agency (FEMA). There was no Trump candidate to head the Transportation Security Administration, and no one to run the Centers for Disease Control and Prevention. The 2020 national census will be a massive undertaking for which there is not a moment to lose, and yet there's no Trump appointee in place to run it. "The actual government has not really taken over," said Max Stier. "It's kindergarten soccer. Everyone is on the ball. No one is at their positions. But I doubt Trump sees the reality. Everywhere he goes, everything is going to be hunky-dory and nice. No one gives him the bad news."

At this point in their administrations, Obama and Bush had nominated their top ten people at the DOE and installed most of them in their offices. Trump had nominated three people and installed just one, former Texas governor Rick Perry. Perry is of course responsible for one of the DOE's most famous moments—when in a 2011 presidential debate he said he intended to eliminate three entire departments of the federal government. Asked to list them he named Commerce, Education, and . . . then hit a wall. "The third agency of government I would do away with . . . Education . . . the . . . ahhhh . . . ahhh . . . Commerce, and let's see." As his eyes bored a hole in his lectern, his mind drew a blank. "I can't, the third one. I can't. Sorry. Oops." The third department Perry wanted to get rid of, he later recalled, was the Department of Energy. In his confirmation hearings to run the department, Perry confessed that when he called for its elimination he hadn't actually known what the Department of Energy did—and he now regretted having said that it didn't do anything worth doing.

The question on the minds of the people who currently work at the department: Does he know what it does now? In his hearings, Perry made a show of having educated himself. He said how useful it was to be briefed by former secretary Ernest Moniz. But when I asked someone familiar with those briefings how many hours Perry had spent with Moniz, he laughed and said, "That's the wrong unit of account." With the nuclear physicist who understood the DOE perhaps better than anyone else on earth Perry had spent minutes, not hours. "He has no personal interest in understanding what we do and effecting change," a DOE staffer told me in June 2017. "He's never been briefed on a program—not a single one, which to me is shocking."

Since Perry was confirmed, his role has been ceremonial and bizarre. He pops up in distant lands and tweets in praise of this or that DOE program while his masters inside the White House create budgets to eliminate those very programs. His sporadic public communications have had in them something of the shell-shocked grandmother trying to preside over a pleasant family Thanksgiving dinner while pretending that her blind-drunk husband isn't standing naked on the dining-room table waving the carving knife over his head.

Meanwhile, inside the DOE building, people claiming to be from the Trump administration appeared willy-nilly, unannounced, and unintroduced to the career people. "There's a mysterious kind of chain from the Trump loyalists who have shown up inside DOE to the White House," said a career civil servant. "That's how decisions, like the budget, seem to get made. Not by Perry." The woman who ran the Obama department's energy-policy analysis unit received a call from DOE staff telling her that her office was now occupied by Eric Trump's brother-in-law. Why? No one knew. "Yes, you can notice the difference," says one young career civil servant, in response to the obvious question. "There's a lack of professionalism. They're not very polite. Maybe they've never worked in an office or government setting. It's not hostility so much as a real sense of concern with sharing information with career employees. Because of that lack of communication, nothing is being done. All policy questions remain unanswered."

The DOE has a program to provide low-interest loans to companies to encourage risky corporate innovation in alternative energy and energy efficiency. The program became infamous when one of its borrowers, the solar energy company Solyndra, was unable to repay its loan, but, as a whole, since its inception in 2009, the program has turned a profit. And it has been demonstrably effective: it lent money to Tesla to build its factory in Fremont, California, when the private sector would not, for instance. Every Tesla you see on the road came from a facility financed by the DOE. Its loans to early-stage solar energy companies launched the industry. There are now thirty-five viable utility-scale, privately funded solar companies—up from zero a decade ago. And yet today the program sits frozen. "There's no direction what to do with the applications," says the young career civil servant. "Are we shutting the program down? There's no staff, just me. People keep bugging me for direction. It's got to the point I don't care if you tell me to tear the program down. Just tell me what you want to do so I can do it intelligently." Another permanent employee, in another wing of the DOE, says, "The biggest change is the grinding to a halt of any proactive work. There's very little work happening. There's a lot of confusion about what our mission was going to be. For a majority of the workforce it's been demoralizing."

Over and over again, I was asked by people who worked inside the DOE not to use their names, or identify them in any way, for fear of reprisal. "People are heading for the doors," says Tarak Shah. "And that's really sad and destructive. The best and the brightest are the ones being targeted. They will leave fastest. Because they will get the best job offers."

There might be no time in the history of the country when it was so interesting to know what was going on inside these bland federal office buildings—because there has been no time when those things might be done ineptly, or not done at all. But if you want to know how the DOE works—the problems it manages, the fears that keep its employees awake at night, the things it does you just sort of assume will continue being done—there's no real point in being inside the DOE. Anyone who wants a blunt, open assessment of the risks inherent in the United States government now has to leave it to find it.

———

By the time I reached John MacWilliams's kitchen table, in Quogue, Long Island, I knew about as much about the DOE as he had when he'd started there, back in 2013. MacWilliams had spent a lot of his life pursuing and obtaining a place in the world that he actually hadn't wanted. In the early 1980s, after graduating from Stanford and Harvard Law School, he took a coveted job at a prestigious New York law firm. Seeing that the action was not in law but in finance, he jumped to Goldman Sachs, where, as an investment banker specializing in the energy sector, he rose quickly. Six years into his career as a Goldman banker, he realized he didn't want to be a banker any more than he'd wanted to be a lawyer. He was actually seriously interested in the energy sector—he could see it was on the cusp of a great transformation—but he didn't particularly care for Wall Street or the effect it was having on him. "One day I looked in the mirror shaving and there was this haggard face and I said, 'But for the money, would you do this?'" What he wanted, he thought, was to be a writer—but when he shared his secret ambition with his Goldman boss, his boss just looked at him pityingly and said, "John, you have to have talent to write a book." He wasn't rich at that point—he had a few hundred grand to his name—but, at the age of thirty-five, he quit his Goldman job and set out to be a novelist.

For the next year he wrote the novel he had imagined—*The Fire Dream*, he called it—and, despite the indifference of the publishing industry, he began another one. But while the first story had come naturally to him, the second one felt forced. He sensed that he probably didn't want to be a writer much more than he had wanted to be a lawyer or an investment banker. "The hardest part was admitting to myself in my black blue jeans that I missed my old life," he said. He set out to raise money for a fund that would invest in energy companies—at which point an editor from Random House called and said he couldn't get *The Fire Dream* out of his head and regretted having rejected it. MacWilliams sensed absurdity in his situation: he'd already abandoned his literary ambition. "I can't be a novelist trying to raise an equity fund," he said, so he stuck his novel back in the drawer and became a founding partner of the Beacon Group, a private investment firm, and also within that group was co-head of a Beacon fund that specifically invested in the energy field. Seven years later he and his partners sold the Beacon Group to JPMorgan Chase for $500 million.

Along the way he'd come to know a nuclear physicist, Ernie Moniz, who asked him to join an MIT task force to study the future of nuclear power. In early 2013, when Moniz was named energy secretary, he called MacWilliams and asked him to come to Washington with him. "I recruited him because my view was you should collect talent," says Moniz. "And it's unusual to have someone willing to work in government who has been so deeply involved in private-sector investment." "I always wanted to serve," says MacWilliams. "It sounds corny. But that's it." Still, he was an odd fit. He'd never worked in government and had no political ambition. He thought of himself as "a problem solver" and a "deal guy." "I'd been investing in energy since the mid-1980s and never once went to the DOE and didn't think I needed to," he said. "I was just wrong."

In the beginning he spent much of his time bewildered.

"Everything was acronyms," he said. "I understood twenty to thirty percent of what people were talking about." He set out, aggressively, to educate himself, pulling people from every nook and cranny and making them explain until he understood what they did. "It took me about a year to understand it all," he said, which inadvertently raises the question of how long it would take someone who wasn't so curious. Anyway, he figured out soon enough that the DOE, though created in the late 1970s, largely in response to the Arab oil embargo, had very little to do with oil and had a history that went back much further than the 1970s. It contained a collection of programs and offices without a clear organizing principle. About half its budget in 2016 went to maintaining the nuclear arsenal and protecting Americans from nuclear threats. It sent teams with equipment to big public events—the Super Bowl, for instance—to measure the radiation levels, in hopes of detecting a dirty bomb before it exploded. "They really were doing things to, like, keep New York safe," said MacWilliams. "These are not hypothetical things. These are actual risks." A quarter of the budget went to cleaning up all the unholy world-historic mess left behind by the manufacture of nuclear weapons. The last quarter of the budget went into a rattlebag of programs aimed at shaping Americans' access to, and use of, energy.

There were reasons these things had been shoved together. Nuclear power was a source of energy, and so it made sense, sort of, for the department in charge of nuclear power also to have responsibility for the weapons-grade nuclear materials—just as it sort of made sense for whoever was in charge of making weapons-grade uranium and plutonium to be responsible for cleaning up their own mess. But the best argument for shoving together the Manhattan Project and nuclear waste disposal and clean-energy research was that underpinning all of it was Big Science—the sort of scientific research that requires multi-billion-dollar particle accelerators. The DOE ran the seventeen national labs—Brookhaven, the Fermi National Accelerator Lab, Oak Ridge, the Princeton Plasma Physics Lab, and so on. "The Office of Science in DOE is not the Office of Science for DOE," said MacWilliams. "It's the Office of Science for all science in America. I realized pretty quickly that it was the place where you could work on the two biggest risks to human existence, nuclear weapons and climate change."

He was surprised—a little shocked, even—by the caliber of civil servants working on these problems. "This idea that government is full of these bureaucrats who are over-paid and not doing anything—I'm sure that in the bowels of some of these places you could find people like that," he said. "But the people I got to work with were so impressive. It's a military-like culture." Federal employees tended to be risk-averse, the sort of people who carry an umbrella around all day when there's a 40 percent chance of rain. But, then, sometimes, they weren't. In 2009, amid protests that helped touch off Libya's bloody civil war two years later, a young woman who worked for him went into the country with Russian security forces and removed highly enriched uranium. The brainpower of those still willing to enter public service also surprised him. "There were physicists everywhere. Guys whose ties don't match their suits. Passive nerds. Guys who build bridges."

Ernie Moniz had wanted MacWilliams to evaluate the DOE's financial risks—after all, that's what he'd done for most of his career—but also, as Moniz put it, to "go beyond financial risks to all the other risks that weren't being properly evaluated." To that end Moniz eventually created a position for MacWilliams that had never existed: chief risk officer. As the DOE's first-ever chief risk officer, MacWilliams had access to everything that went on inside of it and a bird's-eye view of it all. "With a very complex mission and 115,000 people spread out across the country, shit happens every day," said MacWilliams. Take the project to carve football-field-length caverns inside New Mexico salt beds to store radioactive waste, at the WIPP (Waste Isolation Pilot Plant) facility. The waste would go into barrels and the barrels would go into the caverns, where the salt would eventually entomb them. The contents of the barrels were volatile and so needed to be seasoned with, believe it or not, kitty litter. In 2014, according to a former DOE official, a federal contractor in Los Alamos, having been told to pack the barrels with "inorganic kitty litter," had scribbled down "an organic kitty litter." The barrel with organic kitty litter in it had burst and spread waste inside the cavern. The site was closed for three years, significantly backing up nuclear waste disposal in the United States and costing $500 million to clean, while the contractor claimed the company was merely following procedures given to it by Los Alamos.

The list of things that might go wrong inside the DOE was endless. The driver of a heavily armed unit assigned to move plutonium around the country was pulled over, on the job, for drunk driving. An eighty-two-year-old nun cut through the perimeter fence of a facility in Tennessee that housed weapons-grade nuclear material. A medical facility ordered a speck of plutonium for research, and a weapons-lab clerk misplaced a decimal point and FedExed the researchers a chunk of the stuff so big it should have been under armed guard—whereupon horrified medical researchers tried to FedEx it back. "At DOE even the regular scheduled meetings started with 'You're not going to believe this,'" says former chief of staff Kevin Knobloch.

In his four years on the job MacWilliams had come to understand the DOE's biggest risks, the way a corporate risk officer might understand the risks inside a company, and had catalogued them for the next administration. "My team prepared its own books. They were never given to anybody. I never had a chance to sit with the Trump people and tell them what we're doing, even for a day. And I'd have done it for weeks. I think this was a sad thing. There are things you want to know that would keep you up at night. And I never talked to anyone about them."

It's been five months since he left government service, and I'm the first person to ask him what he knows. Still, I think it is important, as I pull my chair in to his kitchen table, to conduct the briefing in the spirit the Trump people might have approached it—just to see how he could have helped even those who thought they didn't need his help. I assume the tone and manner befitting a self-important, mistrustful person newly arrived from some right-wing think tank. And so I wave my hand over his thick briefing books and say, "Just give me the top five risks I need to worry about *right away*. Start at the top."

And right away we have a problem. An accident with nuclear weapons is at the top of his list, and it is difficult to discuss that topic with someone who doesn't have security clearance. But the Trump people didn't have it either, I point out, so he'll just need to work around my handicap. "I have to be careful here," he says. He wants to make a big point: the DOE has the job of ensuring that nuclear weapons are not lost or stolen, or at the slightest risk of exploding when they should not. "It's a thing Rick Perry should worry about every day," he says.

"Are you telling me that there have been scares?"

He thinks a moment. "They've never had a weapon that has been lost," he says carefully. "Weapons have fallen off planes." He pauses again. "I would encourage you to spend an hour reading about Broken Arrows."

"Broken Arrow" is a military term of art for a nuclear accident that doesn't lead to a nuclear war. MacWilliams has had to learn all about these. Now he tells me about an incident that occurred back in 1961, and was largely declassified in 2013, just as he began his stint at DOE. A pair of 4-megaton hydrogen bombs, each more than 250 times more powerful than the bomb that destroyed Hiroshima, broke off a damaged B-52 over North Carolina. One of the bombs disintegrated upon impact, but the other floated down beneath its parachute and armed itself. It was later found in a field outside Goldsboro, North Carolina, with three of its four safety mechanisms tripped or rendered ineffective by the plane's breakup. Had the fourth switch flipped, a vast section of eastern North Carolina would have been destroyed, and nuclear fallout might have descended on Washington, DC, and New York City.

"The reason it's worth thinking about this," says MacWilliams, "is the reason that bomb didn't go off was because of all the safety devices on the bombs, designed by what is now DOE."

The Department of Energy, he continues, spends a lot of time and money trying to make bombs less likely to explode when they are not meant to explode. A lot of the work happens in a drab building with thick concrete walls at the Lawrence Livermore laboratory, in Northern California—one of the three nuclear-weapons research sites funded and supervised by the DOE. There a nice mild-mannered man will hand you a softball-size chunk of what seems to be a building material and ask you to guess what it is. About $10 worth of ersatz marble from Home Depot, you might guess. Whereupon he explains that what appears to be Home Depot marble becomes, under certain conditions, an explosive powerful enough to trigger a chain reaction in a pile of plutonium. The secret that the mild-mannered man would get thrown in jail for sharing is exactly what those conditions are.

That was another thing that surprised MacWilliams when he went to work at the DOE: the sheer amount of classified information. You couldn't really function without being cleared to hear it. There were places in the building where you could share national secrets, and places where you could not. The people from the FBI who had vetted him for his security clearance had made it very clear to him that they would excuse many foibles—affairs, petty crimes, drug use—but they could not excuse even the most trivial deception. They asked a battery of questions on the order of "Have you ever known anyone who has advocated the violent overthrow of the United States government?" They'd asked him to list every contact with foreigners he had had in the past seven years, which was absurd, as he had spent a career in global finance and lived in both London and Paris. But the people who handed out security clearances failed to see the humor in it. They wanted to know everything. There was no way anyone who obtained a security clearance would find it not worth mentioning that, say, he'd recently dined with the Russian ambassador.*

Sitting at his kitchen table with me, MacWilliams picks up his cell phone. "We're a major target of espionage," he says. "You just have to assume that you are being monitored all the time." I look around. We're surrounded by a lot of green Long Island tranquillity.

"By who?" I ask, with what I hope is a trace of scorn.

"The Russians. The Chinese."

---

* See Sessions, Jeff. U.S. attorney general in the Trump administration.

"How?"

"Every phone I have. Every computer."

Outside, on his back lawn, overlooking a lovely estuary, MacWilliams had placed silhouettes of wild beasts to deter Canada geese from landing. I laugh.

"You seriously think someone might be listening to us right now?"

"I may have dropped off their radar," he says. "But you are definitely monitored while you are there."

I check my watch. I have important op-eds to write, and perhaps a few meetings with people who might know people who might know the Koch brothers. If I'm a Trump person I'm going to assume the people in charge of the nuclear weapons are sufficiently alive to the risks around them that they don't need Rick Perry's help. After all, the only thing Trump had to say publicly about Rick Perry during the campaign was that he "should be forced to take an IQ test" and that "he put glasses on so people think he's smart."

"What's the second risk on your list?" I ask.

"North Korea would be up there," says MacWilliams.

Why do I, as an incoming official at the DOE, need to be worried about North Korea?

MacWilliams explains, patiently, that there lately have been signs that the risk of some kind of attack by North Korea is increasing. The missiles the North Koreans have been firing into the sea are not the absurd acts of a lunatic mind but experiments. Obviously, the DOE is not the only agency inside the U.S. government trying to make sense of these experiments, but the people inside the national labs are the world's most qualified to determine just what North Korea's missiles can do. "For a variety of reasons, the risk curve has changed," says MacWilliams guardedly. "The risk of mistakes being made and lots of people being killed is increasing dramatically. It wouldn't necessarily be a nuclear weapon they might deliver. It could be sarin gas."

As he doesn't want to go into further detail and maybe divulge information I am not cleared to hear, I press him to move on. "Okay, give me the third risk on your list."

"This is in no particular order," he says with remarkable patience. "But Iran is somewhere in the top five." He'd watched Secretary Moniz help negotiate the deal that removed from Iran the capacity to acquire a nuclear weapon. There were only three paths to a nuclear weapon. The Iranians might produce enriched uranium—but that required using centrifuges. They might produce plutonium—but that required a reactor that the deal had dismantled and removed. Or they might simply go out and buy a weapon on the open market. The national labs played a big role in policing all three paths. "These labs are incredible national resources, and they are directly responsible for keeping us safe," said MacWilliams. "It's because of them that we can say with absolute certainty that Iran cannot surprise us with a nuclear weapon." After the deal was done, U.S. Army officers had approached DOE officials to thank them for saving American lives. The deal, they felt sure, had greatly lessened the chance of yet another war in the Middle East that the United States would inevitably be dragged into.

At any rate, the serious risk in Iran wasn't that the Iranians would secretly acquire a weapon. It was that the president of the United States would not understand his nuclear scientists' reasoning about the unlikelihood of the Iranians' obtaining a weapon, and that he would have the United States back away foolishly from the deal.* Released from the complicated set of restrictions on its nuclear-power program, Iran would then build its bomb. It wasn't enough to have the world's finest forensic nuclear physicists. Our political leaders needed to be predisposed to listen to them and equipped to understand what they said.

Yeah, well, never mind science—we'll deal with Iran, I could hear some Trump person thinking to himself.

———

By early summer of 2017 I had spoken with twenty or so of the people who had run the department, along with a handful of career people. All of them understood their agency as a powerful tool for dealing with the most alarming risks facing humanity. All thought the tool was being badly mishandled and at risk of being busted. They'd grown used to the outside world not particularly knowing, or caring, what they did—unless they screwed up. At which point they became the face of government waste or stupidity. "No one notices when something goes right," as Max Stier put it to me. "There is no bright-spot analysis." How can an organization survive that stresses and responds

---

* Which is exactly what he did.

only to the worst stuff that happens inside it? How does it encourage more of the best stuff, if it doesn't reward it?

The $70 billion loan program that John MacWilliams had been hired to evaluate was a case in point. It had been authorized by Congress in 2005 to lend money, at very low interest rates, to businesses, so that they might develop game-changing energy technologies. The idea that the private sector underinvests in energy innovation is part of the origin story of the DOE. "The basic problem is that there is no constituency for an energy program," James Schlesinger, the first secretary of energy, said as he left the job. "There are many constituencies opposed." Existing energy businesses—oil companies, utilities—are obviously hostile to government-sponsored competition. At the same time, they are essentially commodity businesses, without a lot of fat in them. The stock market does not reward even big oil companies for research and development that will take decades to pay off. And the sort of research that might lead to huge changes in energy production often doesn't pay off for decades. Plus it requires a lot of expensive science: discovering a new kind of battery or a new way of capturing solar energy is not like creating a new app. Fracking—to take one example—was not the brainchild of private-sector research but the fruit of research paid for twenty years ago by the DOE. Yet fracking has collapsed the price of oil and gas and led to American energy independence. Solar and wind technologies are another example. The Obama administration set a goal in 2009 of getting the cost of utility-scale solar energy down by

2020 from 27 cents a kilowatt-hour to 6 cents. It's now at 7 cents, and competitive with natural gas because of loans made by the DOE. "The private sector only steps in once DOE shows it can work," said Franklin Orr, a Stanford professor of engineering who took a two-year leave of absence to oversee the DOE's science programs.

John MacWilliams had enjoyed success in the free market that the employees of the Heritage Foundation might only fantasize about, but he had a far less Panglossian view of its inner workings. "Government has always played a major role in innovation," he said. "All the way back to the founding of the country. Early-stage innovation in most industries would not have been possible without government support in a variety of ways, and it's especially true in energy. So the notion that we are just going to privatize early-stage innovation is ridiculous. Other countries are outspending us in R&D, and we are going to pay a price."

Politically, the loan program had been nothing but downside. No one had paid any attention to its successes, and its one failure—Solyndra—had allowed the right-wing friends of Big Oil to bang on relentlessly about government waste and fraud and stupidity. A single bad loan had turned a valuable program into a political liability. As he dug into the portfolio, MacWilliams feared it might contain other Solyndras. It didn't, but what he did find still disturbed him. The DOE had built a loan portfolio that, as MacWilliams put it, "JPMorgan would have been happy to own." The whole point was to take

big risks the market would not take, and they were making money! "We weren't taking nearly enough risk," said
MacWilliams. The fear of losses that might in turn be
twisted into antigovernment propaganda was threatening
the mission.

In late June 2017 I went for a long drive in hopes of getting
a clearer picture of risks four and five, which MacWilliams
had gone on to describe for me at greater length—urgent
threats to American life that might just then have been
keeping the leadership of Trump's DOE awake at night,
if there had been any leadership. I started out in Portland,
Oregon, heading east, along the Columbia River.

An hour or so into the drive, the forests vanish and
are replaced by desolate scrubland. It's a startling sight: a
great river flowing through a desert. Every so often I pass
a dam so massive it's as if full-scale replicas of the Department of Energy's building in Washington, DC, had been
dropped into the river. The Columbia is postcard lovely,
but it is also an illustration of MacWilliams's fourth risk:
the electrical grid. The river and its tributaries generate
more than 40 percent of the hydroelectric power for the
United States; were the dams to fail, the effects would be
catastrophic.

The safety of the electrical grid sat at or near the top
of the list of concerns of everyone I spoke with inside
the DOE. Life in America has become, increasingly, reli-
ant on it. "Food and water has become food and water

and electricity," as one DOE career staffer put it. Back in 2013 there had been an incident in California that got everyone's attention. Late one night, just southeast of San Jose, at Pacific Gas and Electric's Metcalf substation, a well-informed sniper, using a .30-caliber rifle, had taken out seventeen transformers. Someone had also cut the cables that enabled communication to and from the substation. "They knew exactly what lines to cut," said Tarak Shah, who studied the incident for the DOE. "They knew exactly where to shoot. They knew exactly which manhole covers were relevant—where the communication lines were. These were feeder stations to Apple and Google." There had been enough backup power in the area that no one noticed the outage, and the incident came and went quickly from the news. But, Shah said, "for us it was a wake-up call." In 2016 the DOE counted half a million cyber-intrusions into various parts of the U.S. electrical grid. "It's one thing to put your head in the sand for climate change—it's like *mañana*," says Ali Zaidi, who served in the White House as Obama's senior adviser on energy policy. "This is here and now. We actually don't have a transformer reserve. They're like these million-dollar things. Seventeen transformers getting shot up in California is not like, 'Oh, we'll just fix the problem.' Our electric-grid assets are growing vulnerable."

In his briefings on the electrical grid, MacWilliams made a specific point and a more general one. The specific point was that we don't actually have a national grid. Our electricity is supplied by a patchwork of not terribly innovative or imaginatively managed regional utilities. The federal government offers the only hope of a coordinated, intelligent response to threats to the system: there is no private-sector mechanism. To that end the DOE had begun to gather the executives of the utility companies, to educate them about the threats they face. "They all sort of said, 'But is this really real?'" said MacWilliams. "You get them security clearance for a day and tell them about the attacks and all of a sudden you see their eyes go really wide."

His more general point was that managing risks was an act of the imagination. And the human imagination is a poor tool for judging risk. People are really good at responding to the crisis that just happened, as they naturally imagine that whatever just happened is most likely to happen again. They are less good at imagining a crisis before it happens—and taking action to prevent it. For just this reason the DOE under Secretary Moniz had set out to imagine disasters that had never happened before. One scenario was a massive attack on the grid on the Eastern Seaboard that forced millions of Americans to be relocated to the Midwest. Another was a Category 3 hurricane hitting Galveston, Texas; a third was a major earthquake in the Pacific Northwest that, among other things, shut off the power. Yet, even then, the disasters they imagined were the sort of disasters that a Hollywood screenwriter might imagine: vivid, dramatic events. MacWilliams thought that, while such things did happen, they were not the sole or even the usual source of catastrophe. What was most easily imagined was not what was most probable. It wasn't the things you think of when you try to think of bad things happening that got you killed, he said. "It is the less detectable, systemic risks." Another way of putting this is: the risk we should most fear is not the risk we easily imagine. It is the risk that we don't. Which brought us to the fifth risk.

When you set out to list the major risks inside a place with a mission as nerve-racking as the DOE's, your mind naturally seeks to order them. One crude way that MacWilliams ordered the 150 or so risks on his final list was to plot them on a simple graph, with two axes. On one axis was "probability of an accident." On the other axis was "consequences of an accident." He placed risks into one of the graph's four quadrants. A nuclear bomb exploding in an assembly plant and blowing up the Texas Panhandle: high consequence, low probability. A person hopping a perimeter security fence at one of the DOE facilities: low consequence, high probability. And so on. Mainly, he wanted to make sure the department was paying sufficient attention to the risks that fell into the graph's most unpleasant quadrant—high probability of an accident/big consequences if it happens. He noticed that many of the risks that fell into this quadrant were giant multi-billion-dollar projects managed by the DOE. MacWilliams coined his own acronym: BAFU. Billions and All Fucked Up.

Anyway, when I had asked him for the fifth risk, he had thought about it and then seemed to relax a bit. The fifth risk did not put him at risk of revealing classified information. "Project management," was all he said.

=====

In December 1938, German scientists discovered uranium fission. Physicist Enrico Fermi's report on the Germans' work made its way to Albert Einstein, and in 1939 Einstein wrote a letter to Franklin Roosevelt. That letter is the founding document of the Department of Energy. By the early 1940s the United States government understood that for democracy to survive it needed to beat Hitler to the atom bomb. There were two ways to build such a bomb—with enriched uranium, or with plutonium. In early 1943, the United States Army was evicting everyone from an area in eastern Washington nearly half the size of Rhode Island and setting out to create enough plutonium for a nuclear bomb. The site of Hanford was chosen in part for its proximity to the Columbia River: the river supplied both cooling water, and electricity. Hanford was also chosen for its remoteness: the army was worried about both enemy attacks and an accidental nuclear explosion. And finally, Hanford was chosen for its poverty. It was convenient that what would become the world's largest public-works project arose in a place from which people had to be paid so little to leave.

From 1943 until 1987, when Hanford closed its last reactor, the place created two-thirds of the plutonium in the United States' arsenal. In that time, it supplied the material for seventy thousand nuclear weapons. What was left behind after the fact was just as astonishing. "Pluto-nium is hard to produce," said MacWilliams. "And hard to get rid of." By the late 1980s the state of Washington had gained some clarity on just how hard. After a long and nasty negotiation, the U.S. government promised to return Hanford to a condition where, as MacWilliams put it, "kids can eat the dirt." More or less overnight Han-ford went from the business of making plutonium to the business of cleaning it up. In its last years as a working factory, the plutonium plant employed around nine thou-sand people. It still employs nine thousand people, and pays them even more than it used to. "It's a good thing that we live in a country that cares enough to take the time it will take, and spend the money it will spend, to clean up the legacy of the Cold War," said MacWilliams. "In Russia they just drop concrete on the stuff and move on." Asked to guess what it might cost the U.S. gov-ernment to return Hanford to the standards now legally required of it, MacWilliams said, "A century and a hun-dred billion dollars." And that, he thought, might be a conservative estimate.

Every year the Department of Energy wires 10 percent of its budget, or $3 billion, into this tiny place. It will likely continue to do so until the radioactive mess is cleaned up. And even though what is now called the Tri-Cities area is well populated and amazingly prosperous—yachts on the river, $300 bottles of wine in the bistros—the abso-lute worst thing that could happen to it is probably not a nuclear accident. The worst thing that could happen is that the federal government loses interest in it and slashes the DOE's budget.* And yet Trump won the county in which Hanford resides by 25 points.

One morning, with a pair of local guides, I drive into the DOE project most direly in need of management. In my lap is a book of instructions for visitors: "Report any spill or release," it says, among other things. "Nobody in the world has waste like ours," says one of my guides as we enter the site. No one has so much strontium 90, for instance, which behaves a lot like calcium and lodges inside the bones of any living creatures it penetrates, basically forever. Along with chromium and tritium and carbon tetrachloride and iodine 129 and the other waste products of a plutonium factory, it is already present in Hanford's groundwater. There are other nuclear waste sites in the United States, but two-thirds of all the waste is here. Beneath Hanford, a massive underground glacier of radioactive sludge is moving slowly but relentlessly toward the Columbia River.

The place is now an eerie deconstruction site, with ghost towns on top of ghost towns. Much of the old plutonium plant still stands: the husks of the original nine reactors, built in the 1940s, still line the Columbia River, like grain elevators. Their doors have been welded shut, and they have been left to decay—for another century. " 'Cold and dark' is a term we like to use," says one of my guides, though he adds that rattlesnakes and other living creatures

---

* As President Trump has proposed to do.

often find their way into the reactors. Of the settlement that existed before the government seized the land, there remain the stumps of trees from what were once orchards and the small stone shell of the town bank. There are older ghosts here, too. What looks like arid scrubland contains countless Indian burial grounds and other sites sacred to the tribes who lived here: the Nez Perce, the Umatilla, and the Yakama. For the 13,000 years or so prior to the white man's arrival, the place had been theirs. To them the American experiment is no more than the blink of an eye. "You have only been here two hundred years, so you can only imagine two hundred years into the future," as a Nez Perce spokesman put it to me. "We have been here tens of thousands of years, and we will be here forever. One day we will again eat the roots." Maybe so. But in 2014 the DOE sent the local tribes a letter to say that, never mind the roots, they shouldn't even eat, more than once a week, the fish they caught in the river.

A young elk gallops across the road in front of our car. Hunting hasn't been allowed on the 586-square-mile tract since 1943, and so there's game everywhere—geese, ducks, cougars, rabbits, elk, and deer. For a shockingly long time, the effects of radiation on living creatures were either ignored or insincerely explored: no one in the frantic race to create nuclear weapons wanted to hear anything that might slow him down. But over the years people who lived downwind of Hanford experienced unusually high rates of miscarriage, certain kinds of cancer, and genetic disorders that went largely ignored. "It's easy to have no observable health effects when you never look," the medical director of the Lawrence Livermore lab said, back in the 1980s, after seeing how the private contractors who ran Hanford studied the matter. In her jaw-dropping 2013 book *Plutopia*, University of Maryland historian Kate Brown compares and contrasts American plutonium production at Hanford and its Soviet twin, Ozersk. The American understanding of the risks people ran when they came into contact with radiation may have been weaker than the Soviets'. The Soviet government was at least secure in the knowledge that it could keep any unpleasant information to itself. Americans weren't and so avoided the information—or worse. In 1962 a worker at Hanford named Harold Aardal, exposed to a blast of neutron radiation, was whisked to a hospital, where he was told he was perfectly okay except that he was now sterile—and *it didn't even make the news*. Instead, Hanford researchers in the late 1960s went to a local prison and paid the inmates to allow the irradiation of their testicles, to see just how much radiation a man can receive before the tails fall from his sperm.

We drive past T plant, the long gray concrete building where they brought the irradiated material from the reactors, to cull the plutonium that went into the bomb that destroyed Nagasaki. Because it, too, is cold and dark, it is of less concern than the land surrounding it, for that is where the waste from the plant got dumped. The Nagasaki bomb contained about 14 pounds of plutonium, but the waste generated fills acres of manicured dirt, the texture of a baseball infield, just downhill from the plant. "The tank farm," they call it. One hundred and seventy-seven tanks, each roughly the size of a four-story apartment building and capable of holding a million gallons of "high-level waste," lay buried on Hanford's tank farms. Fifty-six million gallons in the tanks are classified as "high-level waste."

What, you might ask, is high-level waste? "Incredibly dangerous stuff," says Tom Carpenter, executive director of the Hanford Challenge, an organization that has monitored the site since the late 1980s. "If you're exposed to it for even a few seconds you probably got a fatal dose." And yet as you drive by the tank farms you would never know anything unusual was happening, were it not for the men crawling over it with scuba gear on their backs and oxygen masks on their faces. What we know about them we know mainly from whistle-blowers who worked inside the nuclear facility—and who have been ostracized by their community for threatening the industry in a one-industry town. ("Resistance to understanding a threat grows with proximity," writes Kate Brown.) One hundred and forty-nine of the tanks in the Hanford farms are made of a single shell of a steel ill-designed to contain highly acidic nuclear waste. Sixty-seven of them have failed in some way and allowed waste or vapors to seep out. Each tank contains its own particular stew of chemicals, so no two tanks can be managed in the same way. At the top of many tanks accumulates a hydrogen gas, which, if not vented, might cause the tank to explode. "There are Fukushima-level events that could happen at any moment," says Carpenter. "You'd be releasing millions of curies of strontium 90 and cesium. And once it's out there it doesn't go away—not for hundreds and hundreds of years."

The people who created the plutonium for the first bombs, in the 1940s and early 1950s, were understandably in too much of a rush to worry about what might happen afterward. They simply dumped 120 million gallons of high-level waste, and another *444 billion* gallons of contaminated liquid, into the ground. They piled uranium (half-life: 4.5 billion years) into unlined pits near the Columbia River. They dug forty-two miles of trenches to dispose of solid radioactive waste—and left no good records of what's in the trenches. In early May of 2017 a tunnel at Hanford, built in the 1950s to bury low-level waste, collapsed. In response, the workers dumped truckloads of dirt into the hole. That dirt is now classified as low-level radioactive waste and needs to be disposed of. "The reason the Hanford cleanup sucks—in a word—is shortcuts," said Carpenter. "Too many goddamn shortcuts."

There is another way to think of John MacWilliams's fifth risk: the risk a society runs when it falls into the habit of responding to long-term risks with short-term solutions. "Program management" is not just program management. "Program management" is the existential threat that you never really even imagine as a risk. Some of the things any incoming president should worry about are fast-moving: pandemics, hurricanes, terrorist attacks. But most are not. Most are like bombs with very long fuses that, in the distant future, when the fuse reaches the bomb, might or might not explode. It is delaying repairs to a tunnel filled with lethal waste until, one day, it collapses. It is the aging workforce of the DOE—which is no longer attracting young people as it once did—that one day loses track of a nuclear bomb. It is the ceding of technical and scientific leadership to China. It is the innovation that never occurs, and the knowledge that is never created, because you have ceased to lay the groundwork for it. It is what you never learned that might have saved you.

Toward the end of his time as secretary of energy, Ernie Moniz suggested that the department, for the first time ever, conduct a serious study of the risks at Hanford. Once the risks were spelled out, perhaps everyone would agree that it was folly to try to turn it into, say, a playground. Maybe the U.S. government should just keep a giant fence around the place and call it a monument to mismanagement. Maybe the people at the labs could figure out how to keep the radioactivity from seeping into the Columbia River and leave it at that. Maybe it shouldn't be the DOE's job to deal with the problem, as the problem had no good solution and the political costs of constant failure interfered with the DOE's ability to address problems it might actually solve.

It turned out no one wanted to make a serious study of the risks at Hanford. Not the contractors who stood to make lots of money from things chugging along as they have. Not the career people inside the DOE who oversaw the project and who feared that open acknowledgment of all the risks was an invitation to even more lawsuits. Not the citizens of eastern Washington, who count on the

$3 billion a year flowing into their region from the federal government. Only one stakeholder in the place wanted to know what was going on beneath its soil: the tribes. A radioactive ruin does not crumble without consequences, and yet, even now, no one can say what these are.

Here is where the Trump administration's willful ignorance plays a role. If your ambition is to maximize short-term gain without regard to the long-term cost, you are better off not knowing the cost. If you want to preserve your personal immunity to the hard problems, it's better never to really understand those problems. There is an upside to ignorance, and a downside to knowledge. Knowledge makes life messier. It makes it a bit more difficult for a person who wishes to shrink the world to a worldview.

There is a telling example of this Trumpian impulse—the desire not to know—in a small DOE program that goes by its acronym, ARPA-E. ARPA-E was conceived during the George W. Bush administration as an energy equivalent of DARPA—the Defense Department's research-grant program that had funded the creation of GPS and the internet, among other things. Even in the DOE budget the program was trivial—$300 million a year. It made small grants to researchers who had scientifically plausible, wildly creative ideas that might change the world. If you thought you could make water from sunlight, or genetically engineer some bug so that it eats electrons and craps oil, or create a building material that becomes cooler on the inside as it grows hotter on the outside, ARPA-E was your place. More to the point: ARPA-E was your only place. At any given time in America, there are lots of seriously smart people with bold ideas that might change life as we know it—it may be the most delightful distinguishing feature of our society. The idea behind ARPA-E was to find the best of these ideas that the free market had declined to finance and make sure they were given a chance. Competition for the grants has been fierce: only two out of every hundred have been approved. The people who do the approving come from the energy industry and academia. They do brief tours of duty in government, then return to Intel and Harvard.

The man who ran the place when it opened was Arun Majumdar. He grew up in India, finished at the top of his engineering class, moved to the United States, and became a world-class materials scientist. He now teaches at Stanford University but could walk into any university in America and get a job. Invited to run ARPA-E, he took a leave from teaching, moved to Washington, DC, and went to work for the DOE. "This country embraced me as one of her sons," he said. "So when someone is calling me to serve, it is hard to say no." His only demand was that he be allowed to set up the program in a small office down the street from the Department of Energy building. "The feng shui of DOE is really bad," he explained.

Right away he faced the hostility of right-wing think tanks. The Heritage Foundation even created its own budget plan back in 2011 that eliminated ARPA-E. American politics was alien to this Indian immigrant; he couldn't fathom the tribal warfare. "Democrat, Republican—what is this?" as he put it. "Also, why don't people vote? In India people stand in line in 40 degrees Celsius to vote." He phoned up the guys who had written the Heritage budget and invited them over to see what they'd be destroying. They invited him to lunch. "They were very gracious," said Majumdar, "but they didn't know anything. They were not scientists in any sense. They were ideologues. Their point was: the market should take care of everything. I said, 'I can tell you that the market does not go into the lab and work on something that might or might not work.'"

Present at lunch was a woman who, Majumdar learned, helped to pay the bills at the Heritage Foundation. After he'd explained ARPA-E—and some of the life-changing ideas that the free market had failed to fund in their infancy—she perked up and said, "Are you guys like DARPA?" Yes, he said. "Well, I'm a big fan of DARPA," she said. It turned out her son had fought in Iraq. His life was saved by a Kevlar vest. The early research to create the Kevlar vest was done by DARPA.

The guys at Heritage declined the invitation to actually visit the DOE and see what ARPA-E was up to. But in their next faux budget they restored the funding for ARPA-E.

As I drove out of Hanford, the Trump administration unveiled its budget for the Department of Energy. ARPA-E had since won the praise of business leaders from Bill Gates to Lee Scott, the former CEO of Walmart, to Fred Smith, the Republican founder of FedEx, who has said that "pound for pound, dollar for dollar, activity for activity, it's hard to find a more effective thing government has done than ARPA-E." Trump's first budget eliminated ARPA-E altogether. It also eliminated the spectacularly successful $70 billion loan program. It cut funding to the national labs in a way that implies the laying off of six thousand of their people. It eliminated all research on climate change. It halved the funding for work to secure the electrical grid from attack or natural disaster. "All the risks are science-based," said John MacWilliams when he saw the budget. "You can't gut the science. If you do, you are hurting the country. If you gut the core competency of the DOE, you gut the country."

But you can. Indeed, if you are seeking to preserve a certain worldview, it actually helps to gut science. Trump's budget, like the social forces behind it, is powered by a perverse desire—to remain ignorant. Donald Trump didn't invent this desire. He was just its ultimate expression.

PEOPLE RISK

ALI ZAIDI WAS five years old when his parents moved him from Pakistan to the United States, in 1993. Later he'd marvel at American parents who agonized over the trauma that some trivial relocation—say, from Manhattan to Greenwich, Connecticut—might inflict upon their children. His parents might as well have put him in a rocket and shot him to the moon, and no one made any fuss at all about it. His father wanted to study educational administration ("He loved the idea of helping to run the places people came to learn"), and the one place he knew someone willing to teach him worked at Edinboro University, in northwest Pennsylvania. And so the Zaidis left Karachi, then a city of more than eight million Muslims, for a town of seven thousand Christians. "We went from solidly upper-middle-class to trying to reach into the middle class," recalls Ali. The people in

Edinboro didn't have a lot of money, but Ali sensed that his family had less of it than most. "The other kids pay a dollar-fifty for school lunch and you pay fifty cents—you know something is going on, but you don't really know what." There was no particular reason he needed to figure out what was going on. But, in the most incredible way, he had.

Even as a kid he was interested in politics. That helped. He got that from his parents. "They spent a lot of time talking about society. Good and bad. Justice. About what we owe people," said Ali. In rural Pennsylvania most people were Republicans. Ali became a Republican, too. "I believe in personal responsibility," he said. "It's exciting when people come together because of their faith to do something for their community. To care about something more than themselves." In high school he volunteered for America's Promise Alliance, Colin and Alma Powell's foundation to help poor children. He knocked on doors for the presidential campaign of George W. Bush. He ran track and excelled in the 400-meter dash. He was bright and ambitious and good at school. On a family trip to Boston he got his first, brief glimpse of Harvard and, without giving much thought to how he would pay for it, decided that was where he'd like to go to college. Faculty members at his high school thought Harvard was a bit of a stretch, and they encouraged him to apply to Penn State or the University of Pennsylvania, recalls Ali. He thought they were trying to lower his expectations. In the end he applied to Harvard, and only to Harvard, because, as he put it, "after you applied to one place, why would you waste money to apply to other places?"

Harvard admitted Ali to its class of 2008 and gave him financial aid. Around the same time, the CEO of America's Promise passed through rural Pennsylvania and asked to meet with volunteers. Ali went to a meeting, and one thing led to another: before he knew it Alma Powell, the group's board chairman, asked him to join the America's Promise board. At the time, he thought this was preposterous. The America's Promise board was filled with the biggest names in Republican politics and the CEOs of huge corporations. "I thought it was *crazy*," recalls Ali. "They'd fly me to DC and put me up in a *hotel*."

The Iraq War happened. Guantánamo Bay happened. Hostility toward his fellow Muslims found a greater welcome in his party than elsewhere. Yet Ali remained a Republican. Six or seven months after Hurricane Katrina hit the Gulf Coast he traveled there, with America's Promise, to help. In New Orleans he saw poverty he'd never imagined. "They had to rebuild these schools, and the kids were effusive," he said. "The thing that got me was that they weren't happy because they had just got their school back. They were effusive because suddenly they had a school that worked in the first place." If you had asked Ali, before he went to New Orleans, what he thought of people who didn't help themselves, he would have said, "My parents had to start all over again. What's the big deal? Just suck it up." The sight of little kids post-Katrina jolted him. "It kind of blew my mind—if you are in kindergarten you should at least get a fair shot. It was just eye-opening: to see how much your geography could determine the opportunities available to you."

Now he sensed that poverty came in many flavors. He'd been lucky to have his particular parents and his particular community. He was reminded of the first time he'd run on a track with spikes. "You just fly on the track." The poor kids he saw in New Orleans were trying to run the same race in life that he was. But he was wearing spikes and they weren't. "There's a real idealism that you have to indulge to think that people in New Orleans were now going to pull themselves up by their bootstraps. There were no bootstraps."

He returned to college and rejoined the Harvard Republican Club. The surface of his life remained unchanged. But a new crackling sound in his head made the political program playing there more difficult to hear. One day he attended a debate between his two most famous professors: Michael Sandel, the philosopher, and Greg Mankiw, the economist who had served as chair of George W. Bush's Council of Economic Advisers. "Someone got up and asked, 'If you are a store owner after Katrina, should you hike up the price of flashlights?' Greg Mankiw said yes, without hesitation." Ali remembers thinking: Greg Mankiw is a good guy. But that answer is absolutely wrong. We don't just have markets. We have values. "I started to think, *Ah, man, I'm probably not a Republican*."

A year or so later he listened to a speech by the junior senator from Illinois, Barack Obama. One line from it stuck in Ali's head: "Poverty is not a family value." He worked as a field organizer in Obama's campaign. "The biggest disappointment was that it was a little bit of a cliché: *Harvard liberal*," said Ali. "Whereas my politics before were not a cliché." Two years later he graduated from Harvard, and then Obama was sworn in as president of the United States. Ali knew he had at least a shot at a very junior position in the new administration. "I had for whatever reason in my mind decided that I should go to the place where it wasn't sexy but the sausage came together." That place, he further decided, was the White House's Office of Management and Budget. His first job in the new administration was to take the budget numbers produced by the senior people and turn them into a narrative: a document ordinary people could read.

One day in his new job he was handed the budget for the Department of Agriculture. "I was like, Oh yeah, the USDA—they give money to farmers to grow stuff." For the first time, he looked closely at what this arm of the United States government actually does. Its very name is seriously misleading—most of what it does has little to do with agriculture. It runs 193 million acres of national forest and grasslands, for instance. It is charged with inspecting almost all the animals Americans eat, including the nine *billion* birds a year. Buried inside it is a massive science program, a large fleet of aircraft for firefighting, and a bank with $220 billion in assets. It monitors catfish farms. It maintains a shooting range inside its DC headquarters. It keeps an apiary on its roof, to study bee-colony collapse. There's a drinking game played by people who have worked at the Department of Agriculture: Does the USDA do it? Someone names an odd function of government (say, shooting fireworks at Canada geese that flock too near airport runways) and someone else has to guess if the USDA does it. (In this case, it does.)

A small fraction of its massive annual budget ($164 billion in 2016) was actually spent on farmers, but it financed and managed all these programs in rural America—including the free school lunch for kids living near the poverty line. "I'm sitting there looking at this," said Ali. "The USDA had subsidized the apartment my family had lived in. The hospital we used. The fire department. The town's water. The electricity. It had *paid for the food I had eaten.*"

To prepare for the transition after the 2016 election, the USDA staff had created elaborate briefings for the incoming Trump administration. Their written material alone came to 2,300 pages, in 13 volumes. A lot of people who work in the Department of Agriculture grew up on or around farms. They like to think of the Department of Agriculture as a nice, down-to-earth bureaucracy. They consider themselves more bipartisan, and less ideological, than people at the other federal agencies. "Our plan was to be as hospitable as possible," said one of the transition planners. "We made sure the office space was gorgeous."

To make the Trump people feel at home, the USDA people had set aside the nicest rooms on the top floor of the nicest building, Whitten, with the nicest view of the National Mall. They had fished out of storage the most

beautiful photographs from the USDA's impressive collection and hung them on the walls. They had brought in
computers and office supplies, and organized a bunch of
new workstations. When they heard that Joel Leftwich,
the guy Trump wanted to lead his USDA transition team,
had been a lobbyist for PepsiCo, they brought in a mini-
fridge stocked with Pepsis. That was just the way they
were at the USDA. They didn't think: How the fuck can
people paid to push sugary drinks on American kids be let
anywhere near the federal department with the most influence on what American kids eat? Instead they thought: I
hear he's a nice guy!

No one showed up that first day after the election, or the
next. This was strange: the day after he was elected, Obama
had sent his people into the USDA, as had Bush. At the
end of the second day, the folks at the Department of Agriculture called the White House to ask what was going on.
"The White House said they'd be here Monday," recalled
one. On Monday morning they worked themselves up all
over again into a welcoming spirit. Again, no one showed.
Not that entire week. On November 22, Leftwich made
a cameo appearance for about an hour. "We had thought,
Rural America is who got Trump elected, so he'll have to
make us a priority," said the transition planner, "but then
nothing happened."

More than a month after the election, the Trump transition team finally appeared. But it wasn't a team: it was
just one guy, named Brian Klippenstein. He came from
his job running an organization called Protect the Harvest.

Protect the Harvest was founded by a Trump supporter, an Indiana oilman and rancher named Forrest Lucas. Its stated purpose was "to protect your right to hunt, fish, farm, eat meat, and own animals." In practice it mainly demonized organizations, like the Humane Society, that sought to prevent people who owned animals from doing terrible things to them. They worried, apparently, that if people were forced to be kind to animals they might one day cease to eat them. "This is a weird group," says Rachael Bale, who writes often about animal welfare for *National Geographic.*

One of the USDA's many duties was to police conflicts between people and animals. It brought legal action against people who abused animals, and so maybe it wasn't the ideal place to insert a man who was preternaturally unconcerned with their welfare. The department maintained its composure—no nasty leaks to the press, no resignations in protest—even as Klippenstein focused, bizarrely, on a single issue. Not animal abuse but climate change. "He came in and wanted to know all about the office on climate change," says a former USDA employee. "That's what he wanted to focus on. He wanted the names of the people doing the work." The career staffer running the transition politely declined to give Klippenstein the names, but he said he bore no ill will toward him for asking. Klip—as he became known affectionately—had reassured everyone by saying, to anyone who would listen, that just as soon as this transition was over he was going straight back to his small livestock farm in Missouri. Bless his heart! Everything on the farm was still normal! (And just you never mind why Uncle Joe likes to be alone with his favorite sheep.)

It was obvious to everyone inside the USDA that Klip was in an impossible position; no one person could get his mind around all the things the department did. Just a couple of weeks before the inauguration, Klip was joined by three other Trump people. The four-person team made a show of sitting down with some of the roughly 100,000-person USDA staff to hear what they had to say. These briefings lived up to their name: the entire introduction to the USDA's vast scientific-research unit lasted an hour. "At most of the federal agencies, there were no real briefings," says a former senior White House official who watched the process closely. "They were basically for show. The Trump transition sent in these teams in the end just to say they were doing it."

The Department of Agriculture normally closes for business on Inauguration Day. It's the only federal agency with an office building on the Mall, which, once upon a time, had been the site of an experimental farm. The building is now used as a staging post during the inaugural by the National Guard and the Secret Service. Just before the inauguration, a Trump representative called the USDA and said he wanted the building to remain open, as he was sending thirty-something new people in. Why the sudden rush? Why force the government to turn on the lights and staff the cafeteria and go to the rest of the trouble to animate a federal building on a day no one was working? Even getting people into the building would be difficult, with snipers on the roof and the Metro station closed. A member of the Obama transition team wondered how the newcomers could have been vetted so quickly by the Office of Presidential Personnel. Nine months later, *Politico* published an eye-popping account about these new appointees. Jenny Hopkinson, a *Politico* reporter, obtained the curricula vitae of the new Trump people. Into USDA jobs, some of which paid nearly $80,000 a year, the Trump team had inserted a long-haul truck driver, a clerk at AT&T, a gas-company meter reader, a country-club cabana attendant, a Republican National Committee intern, and the owner of a scented-candle company, with skills like "pleasant demeanor" listed on their résumés. "In many cases [the new appointees] demonstrated little to no experience with federal policy, let alone deep roots in agriculture," wrote Hopkinson. "Some of those appointees appear to lack the credentials, such as a college degree, required to qualify for higher government salaries."

What these people had in common, she pointed out, was loyalty to Donald Trump.

Nine months after they'd arrived, a man I'd been told was the best informed of all the department's career employees about the haphazard transition couldn't tell me how many of these people were still roaming the halls. The few fingerprints they left were characteristically bizarre. They sent certified letters to several senior career civil servants perceived to be close to the Obama administration, telling them they were being reassigned—from jobs they were good at to jobs they knew little about. They instructed the staff to stop using the phrase "climate change." They removed the inspection reports on businesses that abused animals—roadside circuses, puppy mills, research labs— from the department's website. When reporters from *National Geographic* contacted the USDA to ask what was going on with animal-abuse issues, "they told us all of this information was public, except now you had to FOIA it," said Rachael Bale. "We asked for the files, and they sent us seventeen hundred completely blacked-out pages."

By the time I set out to get the briefings the Trump people had not, it was late summer. Of the fourteen senior jobs at the USDA that required Senate confirmation, only one had been filled: former Georgia governor Sonny Perdue was named secretary of agriculture. In April. If Trump's interest in a subject is to be judged by the speed with which he appointed his cabinet secretaries, the Department of Agriculture has a catastrophically tiny share of presidential brain space.

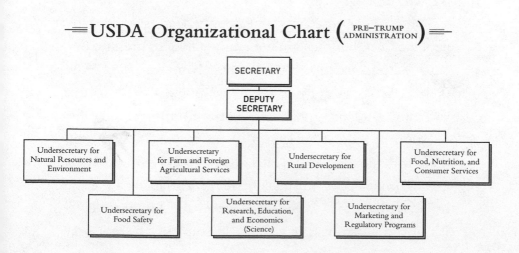

USDA Organizational Chart (PRE–TRUMP ADMINISTRATION)

SECRETARY

DEPUTY SECRETARY

Undersecretary for Natural Resources and Environment

Undersecretary for Farm and Foreign Agricultural Services

Undersecretary for Rural Development

Undersecretary for Food, Nutrition, and Consumer Services

Undersecretary for Food Safety

Undersecretary for Research, Education, and Economics (Science)

Undersecretary for Marketing and Regulatory Programs

At any rate, I'd had a bunch of conversations with people who had run the department under past administrations: former secretaries and deputy secretaries of agriculture. They reached a bipartisan consensus: the best way to get a quick grip on the details of the department is to march through the seven little boxes of its organization chart (see above). For example, if you want to know the likelihood that the geese loitering near the LaGuardia Airport runway will cause your plane to crash-land in the Hudson River and the event will become the subject of a major motion picture, you go to see the undersecretary or deputy under-secretary for marketing and regulatory programs, which oversees the Animal and Plant Health Inspection Service, which handles the bewildering set of conflicts in America between people and animals. (The people tend to get their way.) If you want an up-to-date snapshot of which farmers are most dependent on federal aid, you go see the people who manage the little box marked "Farm and Foreign Agricultural Services."

These undersecretaries and deputy secretaries occupy public offices, but they are not really public figures: no one outside the department knows their names or faces. And their little boxes are not equally exposed to the whims and idiocies of any given presidential administration. The question of the day, at least it seems to me, is: Where in these little boxes is the greatest damage likely to be done, through neglect or mismanagement or malice? Take the little box labeled "Natural Resources and Environment." It's not as abstract as it sounds. It employs around forty thousand people and contains the U.S. Forest Service. Its 193 million acres of forests and grasslands are important to the future of the climate. Its most recent undersecretary, Robert Bonnie, was described to me by one of his superiors as "maybe the single best undersecretary we've ever had." Bonnie himself is a seriously interesting person—and filled with concerns about what the Trump administration might do to his former department. But when I asked him to name his No. 1 concern, he said, "Wildfires."

But if you worry about everything, you wind up worrying about nothing. The Trump administration can forbid federal employees from using the phrase "climate change" more easily than it can prevent them from dealing with its consequences. The career people at the U.S. Forest Service, because they have direct lines into Congress, don't need the White House behind them in the way many other departments do. Fighting wildfires is the most visible thing the USDA does. It's the places in our government where the cameras never roll that you have to worry about most.

Ali Zaidi had been the first to point this out to me: that the seven little boxes inside the Department of Agriculture are not equally vulnerable. And he would know. He'd spent two years as a grunt in the Office of Management and Budget, before moving into ever more important White House jobs. He'd been one of those young people with the gift for getting old people to forget how young he was, and found himself thrust into jobs normally reserved for the middle-aged. In 2014, at the age of twenty-seven, he was put in charge of a team of experts overseeing the Department of Agriculture's entire budget—along with the budgets of the National Aeronautics and Space Administration (NASA), the Department of Energy, the Department of the Interior, the Environmental Protection Agency, and a couple of others. He'd been forced to get his mind fully around the federal department that had underpinned his childhood: it wasn't easy. "Of all the budgets, it's the weirdest," he said. It was weird, first, because the USDA did so many different things. It was weird because so many Americans had no idea how much their lives depended upon it. And it was weird because of the sheer sums of money sloshing around the place, dispensed by government employees no one had ever heard of. If you took a follow-the-money approach to what might go wrong inside the USDA, you ended up inside the box run by Kevin Concannon.

———

I found Concannon at home in the woods of Maine. On the phone he'd told me that he'd spent most of his career running health and nutrition services for several different states. Back in 2008 he'd retired to this place, purchased long ago, with his wife. The woods were near the sea, and so they had bought a small boat. "I was sort of unhappy being retired," he said. "We had the boat. But after two weeks in the boat we said, 'Okay, what are we going to do now?' I don't understand people who say they can't wait to retire. It's like living your life in jail or something." Not long after he'd had that thought, he got a call from the newly appointed secretary of agriculture, Tom Vilsack. "I hired him for several reasons," said Vilsack. "But the first is: heart."

Concannon was pushing seventy, but he came out of retirement to take charge of the box inside the USDA labeled "Food, Nutrition, and Consumer Services." He'd run the place right up until the Trump people finally arrived, in January 2017. In his job at USDA, Concannon had overseen for eight years the nation's school-lunch program; the program that ensures that pregnant women, new mothers, and young children receive proper nutrition; and a dozen or so smaller programs designed to alleviate hunger. Together these accounted for approximately 70 percent of the USDA's budget—he'd spent the better part of a trillion dollars feeding people with taxpayer money while somehow remaining virtually anonymous. "We used to say if we stopped the tourists outside the building and told them what we were doing inside, most of them would have no idea that we were doing it," he said.

He'd helped to prepare for the Trump transition, but, of course, that transition never happened. He hadn't had a single encounter with anyone associated with it. Nor had the Trump people bothered to speak with anyone who reported to him. And so it seemed fair to say, as Concannon had said to me on the phone, that "they don't seem to be focused on nutrition." The Trump people were a bit like those tourists outside the Whitten Building. Only now they were inside it.

Concannon's house is hidden from the road by trees

and so comes as a surprise. So does he: I had expected to meet an old guy with at least some need to convey a sense of his own importance. I expected him to retain at least a trace of the stuffy bureaucrat. Instead I find myself being led through his retirement house by a leprechaun who has disguised himself by shaving his beard. "Media has not been a big part of my life," he says, laughing, as he leads me to a table and chairs out back. "This is new!" Exposed to the early-autumn chill, we play New England's favorite outdoor social game: seeing who will be the first to break and beg to go back inside.

"The food-stamps program," he says, instantly, when I ask him for his biggest concern. The Trump budget had proposed cutting food stamps by more than 25 percent over the next ten years and more or less abandoning the notion that the country should provide some minimum level of nutrition to its citizens. The Trump budget was just an opening bid and unlikely to become policy, at least not right away, because Congress could always fight it. But it signaled an intention and, perhaps, a shift in public attitude. "Why is it that people channel so many of their hang-ups about people who are poor or unsuccessful into the food-stamps program?" asks Concannon as we settle into our chairs, then answers his own question. "No one really knows when you go to the doctor and the government is paying. But people see you with this card or coupon and react. People would say to me, 'I saw someone *buying butter* with food stamps.' And I would say, 'Well, yes.' "

Anyone who takes over his old job, he explains, needs to be especially vigilant about fraud, even though there is probably less of it in the program than ever. Actual fraud in the food-stamp program in 2015 was about 5 percent of the $70 billion paid out. People still succeed in understating their income and get benefits they would otherwise not. People occasionally "traffic," the term of art for exchanging food stamps at less than face value, for cash or ineligible goods. (The storeowner then puts through a bunch of phony purchases, and pockets the difference between what the government pays him and what he has paid to the food-stamper.) And fraud is far more likely in some parts of the country than in others. "The Dakotas—they're all Boy Scouts and Girl Scouts who live there," Concannon says. "But just look at Miami. Or Columbus, Ohio." But replacing food stamps with a card that has a PIN has made fraud, and theft, much less common. The USDA hires specialists to search food-purchase data for suspicious patterns. When they find what appears to be a problem, they send in one of the 100 USDA food-stamp undercover investigators, to gather evidence.

I stop writing and look up. "The Department of Agriculture has private eyes?"

"They're more like Columbos," he says.

But that's not his point, he says. His point is that, while actual fraud is relatively rare, "instances of fraud attract huge media attention and can have big effects—like Surfer Dude." Surfer Dude was a guy in San Diego who claimed on Fox News that the food-stamp program gave him the cushion he needed to surf all day. The network ate it up. And that was the problem: the distorting media coverage of any cheating creates political resistance to the entire enterprise. No one in the Trump administration was likely to ever come right out and say: "We want to let kids and old people go hungry." But, obviously, they might run the program so ineptly that it lost political support. And then kids and old people would go hungry.

What I needed to keep in mind, said Concannon, was just how much was at stake for the people who needed the program. "I used to tell the people that worked for me: You may not ever meet a single person it benefits. You might never see the infants who are fed, or that family that lost a job. To the extent you can keep in mind that they are out there, it will motivate you to do your job better."

It now occurs to me that this question of motivation sits somewhere near the middle of the problem I am investigating. Why does someone go to work inside this little box—or any little box—inside the federal government? There's always an answer to this question. And it's obviously important. Why a person does what he does has a big effect on how he does it. And yet Kevin Concannon, whose little box had spent nearly a trillion dollars, had never really been asked it.

He has an answer to the question, as it turns out. He'd grown up in Portland, Maine, in a working-class family with seven children. His older brother had suffered from schizophrenia. His parents, immigrants from Ireland, had been crippled by the sense that they were responsible for their child's illness. "There was a very strong belief in those days in nurture versus nature," he says. Then one day—like a bolt from the blue—a pair of social workers from the Veterans Administration visited their home. They put his brother on a new medication, which eased his symptoms. "They helped my parents to understand that the fact that he had this illness had nothing whatever to do with how they raised him," says Concannon. "It was luck of the draw."

The effect of these government angels on his family's life was astonishing. By the time Concannon left for college, in 1959, he wondered what it might be like to do that kind of work. In college he read *The Other America*, Michael Harrington's account of the lives of the American poor, and listened to John F. Kennedy's inaugural speech, with its bracing call to public service. By the time he graduated he knew what he wanted to be. Fourteen years later he was running Maine's mental-health services.

He proved effective enough at the job that, after an election pushed him out of it, other states recruited him. In 1987 he took a job running the mental-health and developmental-disabilities programs for Oregon. Four months into his new gig, Oregon's governor, Neil Goldschmidt, grabbed him in the hallway. "He said, 'C'mon to the pressroom. They're naming the new director of human services.' I said, 'Who is it?' And he says, 'It's you!'"

As the head of Oregon's nutrition programs, he learned that the country's willingness to feed people who are hungry does not mean that hungry people are always fed. The federal government makes the benefits available but then leaves it to states to administer them. "Where you live in this country makes a huge difference if you are poor," says Concannon. "And it's not just the weather. You have states with these sixty- or seventy-page documents people have to fill out to get benefits. Poor people are easy to wear down." Georgia was usually a problem. Texas, too. "If they ran any of their football teams the way they run their food program, they'd fire the coach," said Concannon. A Wyoming legislator, proud of how badly he had gummed up the state's nutrition programs, told him, "We pride ourselves on doing the minimum required by the federal government." An Arizona congressman proposed that the card used by people receiving food-stamp benefits be made prison orange, conferring not just nutrition but shame. In 2016, after several counties in North Carolina suffered severe flooding, the state tried to distribute federal disaster-relief food-benefit cards on the day of the presidential election, to give poor people a choice between eating and voting. In Kansas, Concannon had explained to an executive who oversaw the state's food-stamp program how he had made it easier for people in Oregon who were going hungry to access their program. "He said, 'Jeez, if we did that we'd have more people coming in the door.' And I said, 'Yeah, but isn't that the idea?'"

Concannon viewed his job in Oregon simply: to make benefits more easily available to people who qualified for them. Minimize the red tape. Promote the programs. Change the culture that dispensed them from one of suspicion to one of sympathy. From Oregon, at the behest of yet another governor, he returned home to Maine, to run all of the public-health and nutrition programs. There he displayed yet again his unusual gift for finding and slaking need. For instance, he noticed that a lot of people without health insurance in the state were failing to fill their prescriptions, because they couldn't afford the drugs. In northern Maine, people were crossing the border into Canada, where they could buy the same drugs from the same companies at a fraction of the cost. He thought the situation both outrageous and economically inefficient: help people prevent a stroke and you could avoid the far greater expense of caring for them after they had one. He created a program, Maine Rx, that extended the cheaper Medicaid prices of drugs to people who were well above the poverty line. Within three months, 100,000 people had signed up. (The drug companies challenged the program, taking it all the way to the Supreme Court, which mandated some changes. It is now called Maine Rx Plus.)

In 2003, at the request of Iowa governor Tom Vilsack, he left Maine for Iowa. In his six years there, he raised the number of Iowans receiving food stamps by 68 percent.

There was more. But it was getting late.

"Are you cold?" I ask, hopefully.

"No," he says, "but if you are . . ."

We move back inside, to his kitchen table. He locates a plate of freshly baked banana bread and puts it in front of me. I try not to stare at it. Dry banana bread I find inedible. Moist, sticky banana bread I find hard to resist. His banana bread glistens.

There are people who would seek to dismiss his entire enterprise with a single line: Why should my hard-earned dollars go to feed anyone else? They'd see Kevin Concannon as the King of Handouts. A promoter of sloth and indolence.

But the facts of the program he ran for eight years are innocent: its average benefit is just $1.40 cents a meal. Eighty-seven percent of that money goes to households with children, the disabled, and elderly. "The idea that we are going to put these people to work is nonsense." Able-bodied adults on food stamps *are* required to work, or attend job training, for at least twenty hours a week. The nation's private food banks dispense about $8 billion in food each year, while $70 billion in food is provided through food stamps: private charity alone will not feed everyone who needs feeding. The problem with the program is not that people are cheating it. The problem with the program is that people who should be on it are not.

Kevin Concannon had done a lot to fix it: He'd raised the participation rate of the poor people who qualified for it from 72 percent to 85 percent. And he'd reduced fraud rates to all-time lows. But the myths about the food-stamp program—that food stamps can be used in casinos, or to buy alcohol and tobacco, for instance—persisted.

I reach for a slice of banana bread. "Anything else you worried about?" I ask.

"School nutrition," he says, without missing a beat.

One week after being sworn in, Sonny Perdue staged a public event at a school in Leesburg, Virginia. The Obama administration had pushed successfully to raise the nutritional requirements of school meals fed to thirty million American schoolchildren, for the first time in twenty years. To receive federal subsidies for the meals they serve, schools are now required to behave more like responsible parents than indifferent ones: more whole grains, more fruits and vegetables, less sodium, no artificially sweetened whole milk, and so on. Concannon expanded the breakfast programs for kids who did not get fed at home—and that meal, too, became more nutritious. "You can't just serve them pancakes and hot dogs," he says.

Big companies that provided the schools with meals fought back: it was more profitable for them to serve pancakes and hot dogs than fruits and vegetables. But by the end of 2016, America's children were eating better than they had been in 2008. "Ninety-eight percent of the schools were meeting the new standards," says Concannon, "and to those that weren't, that had some problem, we'd say, 'We'll work with you!'"

At the school in Leesburg, Perdue announced that the USDA would no longer require schools to meet the whole-grain standard, or the new sodium standard, or ban fat in artificially sweetened milk. Those changes sound trivial, but the stakes are huge. This is a matter not just of what kind of milk America's schoolchildren drink but also of the process by which we as a society decide which milk they will drink: will it be driven by the dairy industry and the snack-food industry, or by nutritionists?

Concannon was deeply disappointed in Perdue's speech.

He saw it as pure politics, not motivated by any concern for children's welfare. "Look, you can have confidence in the career people," he said. "Because most of them have migrated to where they are out of desire. They believe in what they are doing." About the new political people who might replace him he wasn't so sure. The problem was motive: Why would they come to work at the USDA? A person who worked inside Concannon's little box, as long as they catered to the food industry, could make a lot more money outside of it.

Munching on a second slice of banana bread, I look around Concannon's house. His career was over. He'd spent the better part of fifty years using public money to alleviate suffering. He'd controlled nearly a trillion dollars in government spending. Yet his home is modest. He drives a ten-year-old Volvo. He had gone from state to state, and each time he had been honored for his public service. The plaques were stacked up in his garage. He didn't own enough wall space for them all.

What's striking about Kevin Concannon is what he decided, for whatever reason, he didn't need. He could have named his price with the drug- and food-company lobbies, and yet he'd never taken a job in the private sector. He claims never to have felt the slightest interest in that kind of work. "I've done all right," he says when I ask him, more or less, why he's not rich. "I've always had enough. I've never felt the need to go over to the other side and make three times the amount of money. If you like what you do, you just keep doing it."

On my way out the door he stops me. "You didn't ask me what else I was worried about," he said. "But if you asked me, I'd say science."

━━━━━

The thing you eventually noticed about Cathie Woteki was her detachment. She was slow to talk about the more emotionally charged moments of her career, and even when she did, she didn't talk for long. It wasn't until our fourth conversation, for instance, that she bothered to mention she had become an agricultural scientist only after her professors told her that there was no place for women in basic science. She'd graduated in 1969 from Mary Washington College, the women's affiliate of the University of Virginia, which at the time didn't accept women as undergraduates. From there she followed her future husband to Virginia Tech, where she entered the graduate program in biochemistry. Her fellow graduate students in science were all men. It took her a while to sense how the professors treated her differently from the way they did everyone else. "I finally figured it out when all the guys were given assistantships and I wasn't." She went to the head of the department and asked what she needed to do to get an assistantship, too. "He said I would not be given one because women were a poor investment. I'd probably only have children and drop out."

Looking back, she found it odd that they had let her into the school only to stifle her ambition. But it was the late 1960s, and people were making new, if halfhearted, attempts to address sex discrimination. "If you talk to women scientists of my age, almost all of them have a story similar to mine," she says.

Virginia Tech, like most every college in the United States with "Tech" or "A&M" after its name, was established in the wake of an 1862 law passed by the same Congress that created the Department of Agriculture. In the middle of the Civil War, Lincoln had decided it was time to make U.S. agriculture more efficient: each person not needed on the farm was another person freed up to do something else. That's why the Department of Agriculture was created in the first place, as a vast science lab. Endless statistics illustrate the astonishing effects that lab has had—it has changed the way we live. In 1872, the average American farmer fed roughly four other people; now the average farmer feeds about 155 other people. It's not just people and plants that have become more productive. In 1950, the average cow yielded 5,300 pounds of milk. In 2016, the average cow yielded 23,000 pounds of milk. A Wisconsin Holstein recently yielded nearly 75,000 pounds of milk in a year, which amounts to roughly 24 gallons a day. Her name is Gigi. You can thank her later.

Changes in agricultural science trigger changes in the structure of the society: where people live, what they do, what they value, the metaphors that naturally pop into their minds. Those changes have been driven by research funded by the Department of Agriculture, done inside the land-grant colleges created alongside it. Virginia Tech, like the University of Wisconsin, was one of the original ones. "Because Virginia Tech was a land-grant university, there was a department called Human Nutrition, which I had never heard of as a field of study," says Woteki. She ended up studying the subject because that was what she was encouraged to study. She had no particular connection to farming or agriculture: her father had been an air force fighter pilot; she'd grown up on military bases. "The first time I ever touched a cow," she said, "was when I artificially inseminated one at Virginia Tech."

But she grew interested in the intersection between food and health. Her dissertation investigated a mysterious outbreak of illness in Texas, where, in the late 1960s, Mexican American kids were turning up sick and no one could figure out why. She figured out why: milk. "It wasn't a pathogen," she said. "It was the lactose in the milk." Mexican Americans, as a group, turned out to be especially intolerant of it, though no one had known that until that moment. The symptoms usually started by age eleven or twelve.

She became a professor of human nutrition at an interesting moment: in the early 1970s, Congress was taking a new interest in malnutrition in children. "There was a lot of stunting and wasting in children," she recalls. After a talk given by a congressional staffer studying the effects of legislation on human nutrition, she walked up and introduced herself—and he hired her on the spot. One thing led to another, and soon she was leading a group inside the Department of Agriculture that took survey data and analyzed patterns in food consumption, to explore the relationships between the American diet and American disease. From there she moved naturally enough to the Centers for Disease Control, where she led a team seeking answers to basic questions about the overall health of the population. For instance, blood lead levels in children fell by a lot in the 1970s and early 1980s. This welcome development, they figured out, was due to the phasing out of leaded gasoline.

In early 1993 a pediatrician in Seattle alerted the Washington State Department of Health that he was seeing in children symptoms of *E. coli* such as cramps and bloody diarrhea. In four western states hundreds of people became seriously ill. Four children died. The disease was tracked to Jack in the Box. The chain had been cooking its hamburgers at temperatures too low to kill the bacteria. The Department of Agriculture is responsible for the safety of all meat. The FDA handles all other food. An American killed by his spinach can justifiably blame the FDA, but an American killed by his steak is the responsibility of the Department of Agriculture. Cheese pizzas are the FDA's problem; pepperoni pizzas are supervised by the USDA. After the Jack in the Box outbreak, the USDA created a new little box on the organizational chart called "Food Safety." Woteki became its first undersecretary and served in the post for four years.

After that she thought she was done with government. "Then 9/11 happened," she said. "I had an emotional response: What can I do? It made me realize there were very few people who had ever had the experiences I had

had." She was able to explain the various threats to the food supply as few could, for example. She understood how genetic engineering might be used as a weapon of mass destruction. She knew that a microbe could bring down a civilization. She returned to government. For the last six years of the Obama administration she'd been the Department of Agriculture's chief scientist.

The same qualities that had led her to minimize the importance of her feelings had made her an excellent supervisor of science. Though she didn't seem to care one way or another how she was addressed, no one thought of her as "Cathie." She was always "Dr. Woteki." "She was great at her job," said Tom Vilsack. "She was very adamant about keeping politics out of science. If I called and said, 'How about we delay the announcement of that grant for a week or so,' it was 'Hands off my science!'"

We don't really celebrate the accomplishments of government employees. They exist in our society to take the blame. But if anyone ever paid attention, they would note that Woteki's department, among other achievements, had suppressed the potentially catastrophic 2015 outbreak of bird flu. They'd created, very quickly, a fast new test for the disease that enabled them to cull the sick chickens from the healthy ones. Because of their work, the poultry industry was forced to kill only tens of millions of birds, instead of hundreds of millions. In the early 1990s, the USDA had also dealt with the outbreak of ring-spot virus in papaya trees, when the papaya industry in Hawaii faced ruin and extinction. Inside the little box marked "Science," the USDA helped genetically engineer a papaya tree that was resistant to ring-spot virus.

The worst I could get anyone to say about Cathie Woteki was that she had an unusual sense of humor, at least by the careful standards of the Department of Agriculture. The jokes of scientists sometimes feel like experiments gone wrong, and she was very much a scientist. Her car license plate read DR WO. No one at the USDA called her that, or could imagine doing so. At Secretary Vilsack's small office Christmas dinner for top USDA officials, Cathie's scientist husband came wearing an elf hat. "No one knew why," says a USDA staffer. "She had looked at her husband dressed as an elf and said, 'Yep, that'll work.' She never explained it. It was actually kind of endearing."

The first time we spoke wasn't long after Trump had nominated her replacement. His name was Sam Clovis. He had a doctorate in public administration from the University of Alabama but no experience in science. He'd come to prominence in 2010 as a Rush Limbaugh–style right-wing talk-radio host in Sioux City, Iowa. As Iowa chairman of Rick Perry's 2016 presidential campaign, he'd ripped Trump loudly and righteously for having "no foundation in Christ." Then he'd quit Perry's campaign to become co-chairman of the Trump campaign, declining to address rumors he'd done it for the money. ("I'm not going to talk about how much money I'm getting paid," he told the *Des Moines Register*. "It's just not going to happen.") His appointment as the USDA's chief scientist felt like a practical joke to those who had worked there: this was the place that, back in the early 1940s, had taken Alexander Fleming's findings and effectively invented penicillin. It had triggered the antibiotics revolution. It had coped with blights and outbreaks. The consequences of the science it funded—or did not fund—was mind-boggling. The person Clovis was replacing had taught at universities, worked in the White House, and, along the way, been elected to the National Academy of Sciences.

"They are going to politicize the science," said Woteki. "My biggest concern is the misuse of science to support policies."

In recent years, much of the department's research has dealt with the effects of climate change. The head of science directs nearly $3 billion in grants each year. Woteki directed the science that leads to nutritional standards for schoolchildren. She set research priorities. Hers had been food security; domestic and global nutrition; safety of the food supply; and figuring out how best to convert plants into fuel. "All of that has to be done in the face of a changing climate," said Woteki. "It's all climate change." It might sound silly that the USDA funds a project that seeks to improve the ability of sheep to graze at high altitudes—until you realize that this may one day be the only place sheep will be able to graze. "We're going to become even more reliant on the efficiencies that come from the investment in science," she said. One-quarter of the arable land in the world is already degraded, either by overfarming or overgrazing. "Changing temperatures and changing rainfall patterns will force changes in the way crops are grown and livestock are raised," she said. "The changing climate brings new risks of food-borne disease. Even the pathogens are influenced by temperature and humidity."

If the Trump administration were to pollute the scientific inquiry at the USDA with politics, scientific inquiry would effectively cease. "These high-level discussions really worry me," she says. Research grants will go not to the most promising ideas but to the closest allies. "There is already good science that isn't being funded," she said. "That will get worse." Junk science will be used to muddy issues like childhood nutrition. Maybe sodium isn't as bad for kids as people say! There's no such thing as too much sugar! The science will suddenly be "unclear." There will no longer be truth and falsehood. There will just be stories, with two sides to them.

Since she had run two of the little boxes on the org chart, I decided to kill two birds with one stone and ask Woteki what most worried her about food safety.

"Regulatory reform in food safety without science," she said.

That was too general. I pressed her for some real, specific concern. "They could increase the line speeds," she said, without having to think.

The USDA has big, fat, quite readable rule books to prevent meat from killing people. One rule concerns the speed of the poultry-slaughter lines: 140 birds a minute. In theory, some poor USDA inspector is meant to physically examine each and every bird for defects. But obviously no human being can inspect 140 birds a minute.

No industry can kill nine billion birds each year without wanting to find faster ways to do it. In the fall of 2017, the National Chicken Council petitioned the USDA to allow for line speeds of 175 or faster. "It'll make it even harder for inspectors to do their jobs," says Woteki. (The petition, at least for now, stands rejected.)

What she fears isn't so much the bad intentions of the people who fill the jobs she once did. She fears their seeming commitment to scientific ignorance. No big chicken company wants to poison a bunch of children with salmonella. But if you speed up the slaughter lines, you need to make the new speed safe. Ignorance allows people to disregard the consequences of their actions. And sometimes it leads to consequences even they did not intend.

Ali Zaidi drew a distinction between the little boxes inside the Department of Agriculture that enforced regulation (such as Food Safety) and those that spent money (such as Science). "One is the stick and the other is the carrot," he said. "You pay for things often that you can't or won't regulate." Where the government had the power to regulate, it had less need to pay for things. It couldn't compel university professors to do agricultural research, and so it paid them to do it. It had the power to compel, say, egg producers to adhere to rules that kept eggs from making people sick, and so didn't need to pay them to do it. "In the extreme case the federal government could just buy eggs for everyone and test all of these eggs," said Zaidi. "That's obviously a dumb thing to do from an economic point of view, but it shows you how regulation takes the place of expenditure."

The regulation side of things is, as a rule, less vulnerable to the short-term idiocy of a new administration than the money side of things. The big show Trump has made of removing regulations by executive order has done far less than he suggests, as there is a formal rule-changing process: you must solicit outside opinion, wait a certain amount of time for those opinions to arrive, and then deal with the inevitable legal challenges to your rule change. To increase the number of chickens a poultry company murders each minute might take years, even if it is the smart thing to do.

But to change who gets money to do agricultural research, or whether they get it at all, is a cinch. For that reason, Ali thought the little box marked "Science" was of far greater concern than the box marked "Food Safety."

There were two other important little boxes inside the USDA. One was marked "Farm," and the other was "Rural Development." Ali Zaidi had watched many billions flow through the first and a few billion flow through the second. He thought it highly unlikely the Trump administration's budget cuts would have much effect on the farm dollars. A lot of that money went to big grain producers. The same Republican senators from farm states who said they abhorred government spending of almost any sort became radical socialists when the conversation turned to handouts to big grain producers. "The money follows the political power of the constituencies," said Ali, "instead of the evidence of need in America. If you really boil down the difference between the farm side of the budget and the rural-development side of the budget, the farm subsidies can wind up in the pockets of large corporations. It's the rural-development money that tends to stay in these communities."

Without that money, he thought, rural America would be a very different place than it is. "Without the USDA money it's possible we'd look like sub-Saharan Africa, or rural China," said Ali. Much of small-town America is dispersed and disorganized and poor. The people in those communities don't have the money to hire Washington lobbyists. Yet a way of life depends on the sort of federal subsidies only a powerful lobbyist might procure. "It's preserving an emotional infrastructure," said Ali. "We have decided this is the type of community we want to preserve. But the entire time I was in the White House, we grappled with the question: Where do we find the political capital for rural development? Because it can't just come from the people rural development helps."

———

By the time she left the little box marked "Rural Development," Lillian Salerno had spent the better part of five years inside it. The box's function was simple: to channel low-interest-rate loans, along with a few grants, mainly to towns with fewer than fifty thousand people in them. Her department ran the $220 billion bank that serviced the poorest of the poor in rural America: in the Deep South, and in the tribal lands, and in the communities, called *colonias*, along the U.S.-Mexico border. "Some of the communities in the South, the only checks going in are government checks," she said. And yet, amazingly, they nearly always repaid their loans.

Half her job had been vetting the demands from rural America for help. The other half had been one long unglamorous road trip. "It wasn't like I could just fly to New York City. I'd be going to, like, Minco, Oklahoma. Everywhere I went was two flights minimum plus a two- or three-hour drive." On the other end of the trip lay some small town in dire need of a health center, or housing, or a small business. "You go through these small towns and you see these ridiculously nice fire stations. That's us," she said. It was always more expensive for these towns to get electricity and internet access and health care. "But for the federal government, rural Alaska wouldn't have any drinking water." The need was incredible; her work felt urgent. "We'd give forty thousand dollars for a health clinic and the whole time you're like, Shit, this makes a difference."

As the USDA's loans were usually made through local banks, the people on the receiving end of them were often unaware of where the money was coming from. There were many stories very like the one Tom Vilsack told, about a loan they had made, in Minnesota, to a government-shade-throwing, Fox News–watching, small-town businessman. The bank held a ceremony and the guy wound up being interviewed by the local paper. "He's telling the reporter how proud he is to have done it on his own," said Vilsack. "The USDA person goes to introduce herself, and he says, 'So, who are you?' She says, 'I'm the USDA person.' He asks, 'What are you doing here?' She says, 'Well, sir, we supplied the money you are announcing.' He was white as a sheet."

Salerno saw this sort of thing all the time. "We'd have this check," said Salerno. "We'd blow it up and try to have a picture taken with it. It said UNITED STATES GOVERNMENT in great big letters. That was something that Vilsack wanted—to be right out in front so people knew the federal government had helped them. In the red southern states the mayor sometimes would say, 'Can you not mention that the government gave this?'" Even when it was saving lives, or preserving communities, the government remained oddly invisible. "It's just a misunderstanding of the system," said Salerno. "We don't teach people what government actually does."

She herself hadn't learned until very late. She'd grown up in a family with no money, and nine children, and Republican sympathies, in a small farming town in Texas called Little Elm. Her graduating high school class had eighteen people in it. She was both student council president and head cheerleader. ("The reason I'm not very good at math is you had to choose: cheerleading or math. And I chose cheerleading.") Few of her school's graduates ever went to college, but she was admitted to the University of Texas, on a Pell grant. She paid for what the grant didn't by waiting tables.

She was waiting tables in Little Elm in the late 1980s when friends started getting sick, and dying, from AIDS. She went to Dallas to visit them. There, at a hospital, she saw that men condemned to death were going without care: the nurses were frightened to interact with them. They had a particular fear of being infected by the needles that delivered medication to the patients. "At that time everyone died," said Salerno. "And they are told, 'The nurses aren't coming.' I said, 'That's about as fucked as anything I ever saw.'" She had a raw sense of injustice, and a desire to see life be made fair. "Small town, big family, no resources: you look at the world in a certain way." She also had a roll-up-your-sleeves-and-fix-it attitude. After seeing the needless suffering, she came up with an idea: the retractable needle. It worked like a ballpoint pen. A friend of hers, an engineer, designed it. She applied to the local community bank for a loan and got it. It wasn't until much later that she discovered that the loan had ultimately come from the Small Business Administration, and that the federal government had simply used the local bank as a delivery system. She didn't know enough to know that no bank was going to lend money to a first-time entrepreneur on the strength of a new invention—in part because banks didn't value willpower. "All good inventions come from something personal," she said. "People create things because it's personal."

Salerno and her partner built and ran the new company in Little Elm and called it Retractable Technologies. They received their first patent in the early 1990s and FDA approval in 1997. The first year in business they sold one million syringes, the next year three million. By the third year her company employed 140 people in Little Elm. She repaid the bank her government loan—and she still didn't realize it was a government loan. For the first time in her life she had money.

She also now had a view of the inner workings of the health care industry. The company that had made the old syringes, Becton, Dickinson & Co., controlled more than 80 percent of the market and felt threatened. It wasn't long before Becton started to require hospital systems to buy its clumsy new version of a safe syringe, by bundling it with other products. Salerno assumed Becton was counting on her inability to pay for the lawsuits required to fight them. But she did and wound up with a settlement of $100 million in 2004.

Even then, Becton found ways to keep her new product from gaining full access to the market. Her company survived but didn't become what it might have. It now employs 130 people, instead of the 200 at its peak. Salerno concluded that increased corporate power was one of the forces that had reduced the opportunity available in rural America. The rapacity of companies with monopolistic power, and their ability to have their way with the government, got her thinking about the big American systems. "The entire health industry lies about what things cost to make," she said. "I know what things cost because I made them."

Her outrage led her to support Hillary Clinton's presidential campaign in 2007, but she soon switched to Obama. ("I switched because I got so angry at how they were beating him up.") After Obama won, Salerno was a natural candidate for a job she had no idea existed: helping people in rural America to help themselves. "Someone said, 'Why don't you become an administrator in rural America, at the Department of Agriculture?' I said, 'There's an administrator in rural America?'"

She'd come to her job inside the little box marked "Rural Development" without any particular ambition to be there. The sums of money at her disposal were incredible: the little box gave out or guaranteed $30 billion in loans and grants a year. But people who should have known about it hadn't the first clue what it was up to. "I had this conversation with elected and state officials almost everywhere in the South," said Salerno. "Them: We hate the government and you suck. Me: My mission alone put $1 billion into your economy this year, so are you sure about that? Me thinking: We are the only reason your shitty state is standing."

She was a small-business person first and had no affection for the inefficiencies she found inside the federal government. "You have this big federal workforce that hasn't been invested in forever," she said. "They can't be outward-facing. They don't have any of the tools you need in a modern workplace." She couldn't attract young people to work there. Once, she tried to estimate how many of the USDA's 100,000 employees had been taught how to create a spreadsheet. Fewer than fifty people, she decided. "I was always very aware how we spent money. When I would use words like 'fiduciary duties' or say, 'Those are not our dollars,' they would say, 'Are you sure you aren't a Republican?' But I was really sensitive to the fact that this wasn't our money. This was taxpayer money. This was money that had come from some guy working for fifteen bucks an hour."

The big messy federal government was still the only tool for dealing with what she saw as a growing crisis: the deconstruction of rural America. "It's hard to quantify what it means not to have your entire town's businesses shuttered up because Walmart moved there," she said. There was a hole in the American capital markets: they simply didn't reach small towns. And there were lots of stats that suggested that society benefited from having small towns—and that small-town life made some important, perhaps undervalued, contributions to the whole. Fifteen percent of the country lives in towns of fewer than 10,000 people, for instance, but a far greater proportion of the armed services come from rural areas than from urban ones.

But the more rural the American, the more dependent he is for his way of life on the U.S. government. And the more rural the American, the more likely he was to have voted for Donald Trump. So you might think that Trump, when he took office, would do everything he could to strengthen and grow the little box marked "Rural Development." That's not what has happened.

The Trump administration wanted to show early that it was serious about foreign trade. This desire expressed itself in the Department of Agriculture by a splitting of the little box marked "Farm and Foreign Agricultural Services" into two little boxes—one for farm programs and another for Foreign Agricultural Affairs, or trade. Oddly, at that very moment, Trump was removing the United States from the Trans-Pacific Partnership and costing American farmers an estimated $4.4 billion a year in foreign sales, according to the American Farm Bureau Federation. As there's a rule against having more than seven little boxes on the USDA's org chart, they had to eliminate one of the little boxes. The little box they got rid of was Rural Development. "I worked in the little box in the government most responsible for helping the people who elected Trump," said Salerno. "And they literally took my little box off the organization chart."

This troubled Lillian Salerno, and not just because she'd spent five years of her life inside that little box. It troubled her because it made her wonder about the motives of the people who had taken over the Department of Agriculture. She'd worked inside the little box for a reason. And if you wanted to understand what was at stake inside these little boxes, you could not neglect the motives of the people who ran them. "You want to know what worries me most?" she says after I ask her the question I'd come to ask her. "I am absolutely convinced about one thing: there are conversations going on right now in New York and Washington between people in the Trump administration and Wall Street bankers about how to get their hands on the bank portfolio. Folks in banking: I'm sure they are nice people—they just can't help themselves."

She's worried that an only partially adequate tool for

helping people who were raised in the country's unlucky places will be turned into a source of profits for the biggest financial firms. She thinks that was why they eliminated her little box and moved the $220 billion bank into the office of the secretary: so they could do new things with the money without people noticing. "At the end of the day, what do I think they are going to do?" she said. "Take all the money and give it to their banker friends. Do things like privatize water—so people in rural Florida will be paying seventy-five dollars a month for it instead of twenty dollars."

Lillian Salerno had observed the Trump administration for a long moment. Virtually all the people Trump had sent into the Department of Agriculture were white men in their twenties. They exhibited no knowledge of, or interest in, the problems of rural Americans. She decided there was only one thing to do: move back to Texas and run for office. She had no illusions about herself as a political candidate. She was still a small-town girl from Little Elm, Texas. "I'm still basically a waitress," she said. "I still feel like this. If I get to be a congressman, I'll still feel like that." Ali Zaidi had asked a question: Where would the political capital come from to help people in rural America? Well, it would come from her.

Zaidi marveled at how hard it was for Americans to see the source of their society's strength. People who came to the United States from other countries had this one advantage: they didn't take it for granted. "The immigrant journey has a time compression to it," he said. "Within a generation you're able to see how the rungs of the ladder of opportunity are laid out in front of you, and you can see the hands that pull you up. You see people pull you up and you say, 'Okay, I've got to do the same thing for other people.' I came up that ladder of opportunity, but even I didn't know the names of the government programs that made up the ladder itself. Growing up, what was obvious to me was the kindness of community members. But government was less visible. You need to work really hard to appreciate it."

And who wants to do that?

|||

ALL THE
PRESIDENT'S
DATA

A S SHE WALKED the path that the tornado had torn through the American town, she was struck by how hard it would have been to imagine what she was now seeing. Two days earlier, on May 22, 2011, the wind had cleaved Joplin, Missouri, in two, leaving behind a lot of you-have-to-see-it-to-believe-it stuff: a rubber hose run entirely through a tree trunk; a chair sideways, all four legs piercing a wall; a giant Walmart tractor trailer thrown two hundred yards onto the top of what had been the Pepsi building; a full-size SUV folded in half around a tree. The metal had been flayed from the car, and the tree was no longer a tree but a tree trunk, as all the branches had snapped and blown away. "I felt like some giant had taken an egg beater and run it through a town," said Kathy Sullivan. "It was toothpicks."

Then she realized that the egg beater metaphor was not

exactly right, as the edges of the destruction were eerily undisturbed. What the tornado had narrowly missed was as perfectly preserved as what it had hit was perfectly elim- inated. "It was like when you run your finger through the icing on top of a cake," she said. "A clean line of total destruction." Doctors in the local emergency rooms were seeing trauma they'd never seen. Body parts strewn on the ground outside the hospital. A small child, back stripped of flesh right down to the bone: they could count his vertebrae. People impaled by street signs. People with wounds that looked as if they were caused by automatic rifles—except that the objects deep inside them were not bullets. Seriously injured people had driven themselves to the hospital with dead loved ones in their cars and apologized to the hospital staff. They didn't know what else to do with the bodies.

Tornado outbreaks in the middle of the United States that spring had killed more than five hundred people. In Joplin alone 158 people had died, and thousands had been injured, many critically. That was more than had been killed by a single tornado since the U.S. government had taken on the job of warning people about them. In and of itself this was shocking, but to Kathy Sullivan it was espe- cially so. These people had been informed; the warnings from the National Weather Service, which would soon be reporting to her, had been even better this time than they usually were. The initial tornado watch had come four hours before the event—but then a tornado watch is different from a tornado warning. The average National Weather Service tornado warning comes thirteen minutes before a tornado strikes: Joplin's sirens had sounded the warning seventeen minutes before the tornado touched down and nineteen minutes before it entered Joplin. But the citizens of Joplin had ignored it. "*The majority of surveyed Joplin residents did not immediately go to shelter upon hearing the initial warning. . . ,*" as the report Sullivan would soon oversee noted.

———

One day someone will write the history of the strange relationship between the United States government and its citizens. It would need at least a chapter on the government's attempts to save the citizens from the things that might kill them. The first successful tornado prediction was made on an air force base in Norman, Oklahoma, in 1948. The men who made it had been lucky: they wouldn't be able to do it again. Knowing this, the government had taken the view that people were better off not being warned. The Weather Bureau, as it was then called, was banned from using the word "tornado." It just frightened people, the bureau believed. But word got out: the government meteorologists had this mysterious new skill. And people *demanded* to hear what they had to say, even if what they had to say was of little value.

Since then, the government meteorologists had gotten better at their jobs. The billions of dollars they'd spent on satellites, radar, computing power, and better forecast models had led to, among other things, truly useful tornado warnings. And yet people didn't seem to realize that the government's weather information was more and more reliable—or even that it was their government giving it to them. It no longer shocked Kathy Sullivan to hear otherwise educated citizens say that they got their weather from the Weather Channel. Or some app on their phone. A United States congressman had asked her why the taxpayer needed to fund the National Weather Service when he could get his weather from AccuWeather. *Where on earth did he think AccuWeather—or the apps or the Weather Channel—got their weather?* Where was AccuWeather when winds of two hundred and something miles per hour were churning through an American town, killing people?

Clearly, citizens didn't understand their government. But that had been true for some time. Now Kathy saw that the government didn't really understand its citizens, either. Why had they not saved themselves? If anyone should know the answer to that question, it was Kathy herself—and she had no clue. In some curious way, the United States government had a better handle on the weather than on its own people. It had spent billions of dollars to collect data about the weather, and none about how people responded to it.

She could not help but admire the people of Joplin. Walking through the ruins, she saw all over again what she had seen so many times: how much better Americans were at responding to a disaster than preventing it. Everybody who could was pitching in to help. The border of the devastated area looked like a tailgater at a college football game. The people who had been spared were cooking food for the people who had not. "No one asked questions," said

Kathy. "No one asked if your home had been destroyed. If you walked up and said you were hungry, you got food."

No one could say she hadn't done her job. She was not by nature or upbringing a political person, but her ambition had led her to become one. She had made all the little compromises—done all the little deals with others and with herself—required to survive in the upper reaches of American government. She was now second-in-command—and soon to be first—at the National Oceanic and Atmospheric Administration, or NOAA. NOAA oversaw the National Weather Service, among other things. The National Weather Service had seen the tornado and had issued a warning. Her people had given these people what they needed to survive. And yet on May 22, 2011, more Americans had been killed by a single tornado than on any day in the past sixty-four years.

She might have said nothing. Just thrown up her hands in the privacy of her office and told herself that it wasn't her job to save people from their own stupidity. Instead she asked herself: *What don't we understand about our own citizens?* She flew back to Washington and gathered the relevant parties—all of whom might have claimed credit for a job well done—and asked them, "Is anyone here happy about the outcome?"

To their credit and hers, no one was.

Before she had been given her first paying job by the United States government, Kathy Sullivan had been put through a battery of tests. Some were physical, some were psychological, and others—well, she didn't know quite what they were. At no point during them had she figured out what her testers were looking for. She survived two virtually identical interviews with the National Aeronautics and Space Administration, one with a good NASA cop, the other with a bad NASA cop. "The bad cop made you feel uncomfortable," she said. "The room was ill-lit. He sat behind the desk, and you sat in an exposed chair. You weren't facing each other. He was mumbling and not friendly. Then they did it all over again with a warm, sunny guy who was your best friend." Only much later did she learn that they wanted to see if she answered questions the same way whether she was at ease or not. "I didn't have anything to compare it to," she said. "You might try to manipulate the system, but you need to know the system, and I didn't."

Later she decided that they weren't even really trying to figure out who she was. All they had wanted was the answer to a question: Will she be that same person that she appears to be now when she is traveling at 17,500 miles per hour 140 miles above Earth and something goes bang?

This was her first job interview, and she was applying to be an astronaut. It was 1977, but the work was still risky. "Every flight was still proving that you can get up there and come back alive," she said. "It's like riding bombs." Still, 8,078 other Americans had applied for the job. Five thousand six hundred eight of these had satisfied the basic job requirements. Of those, NASA invited 208 people to the Johnson Space Center, outside Houston, for a week of interviews. "They interviewed us in groups of twenty," Kathy said. "I got there and saw this cluster of other people. It was all guys. That was okay. I'd been the only woman in a field camp and the only woman on a ship." The difference was that this wasn't just guys but a club. "My sense was a lot of these guys knew each other. They're fighter pilots or whatever. I'm twenty-five. I'm a grad student. I'm broke. They seem to be settled in and knew what they're doing—and I didn't. I thought, *Well, Kathryn, enjoy the week.*"

The main event was a ninety-minute interview at a long table filled with strangers. One was the famously inscrutable head of the astronaut program, George Abbey. At the start he leaned back in his chair, eyes half-closed, and did not so much ask as mutter, "Tell us about yourself. Start with high school." That was it. Nothing more. "It was deliberately underspecified," Kathy said.

Telling people about herself wasn't her strong suit. "I've never been a self-revealing person," she said. She went ahead and told them about herself anyway. How by the age of thirteen she'd learned from her father, an aerospace engineer, to fly a plane. How, as a girl growing up in the fifties and sixties, she assumed that her ticket to adventure was not a pilot's license but her gift for languages. Before she graduated from high school, without setting foot in France or Germany, she became fluent in both French and German. She planned to learn a bunch more languages. "My simple theory was: learn lots of languages and use them to see the world," she recalled, in an oral history for the Johnson Space Center. She entered UC Santa Cruz in 1969 as a language major. But there was a science requirement, and to fulfill it she took two classes in ocean science. There she learned that human beings were now descending fourteen thousand feet in tiny submarines and *mapping* the ocean floor. "It was endlessly fascinating. This mix of things I'd always seen on the pages of *National Geographic.*"

The travel she'd imagined until then had been horizontal: east or west, north or south. She now began to imagine it as vertical, too: up and down. She wanted to study the plates beneath the bottom of the sea.

She was accepted into graduate geology programs everywhere she applied, including Princeton, with full research fellowships. She accepted the free ride at Dalhousie University, in Halifax, Nova Scotia, because what interested her was the mountain range at the bottom of the Atlantic Ocean known as the mid-ocean ridge, and for several reasons Nova Scotia seemed to her the best place to study it. From just about the moment she arrived, she started looking for access to a submarine that could take her down, so that she might inspect the mid-ocean ridge up close. "I'm pursuing an academic career and asking, 'How do I get into one of those submarines?' I wanted to go see the stuff myself."

It was her brother who had first told her about NASA's new need for astronauts. He'd seen an ad in the newspaper announcing that the space agency was opening its rocket ships to all Americans between the ages of twenty-five and forty, under six feet tall, weighing less than 180 pounds, and in possession of just about any sort of college science degree. He'd already applied and thought she also should. Women were specifically encouraged for the first time. Minorities, too. All that was required were some character traits: "a willingness to accept hazards comparable to those encountered in modern research airplane flights, a capacity to tolerate rigorous and severe environmental conditions, and an ability to react adequately under conditions of stress or emergency." Up to that moment NASA had been looking mainly for test pilots who could at least feign indifference to their mortality. Now they were looking for scientists—or at any rate scientifically minded people—but with a twist: they needed the temperament of fighter jocks. Kathy hadn't taken her brother seriously. *You really think they're going to hire an oceanographer? A girl????*

A few weeks later she ran across the call for astronauts again, this time in a science journal. They really did seem to want women scientists. And she sensed that she might be the sort of woman they were looking for. "I never brought normal girl books home from the library," she recalled. "I was fascinated by maps and the stories they told." She was handy, too, and quick to figure out how things worked. "I kind of always flunked the dolls test," she told an interviewer for the Johnson Space Center's oral history project. "I never found the dolls interesting. The doll*house* stuff I found interesting, but from an architectural point of view: *building* them. And I'd want to lay them out differently. I didn't want to just move the furniture around, and I sure didn't want to just sit there and imagine conversations [between dolls] that never happened. Let me go build another house; that was more interesting."

The head of NASA's astronaut program had asked her to tell the group about herself—but she sensed that they were after something else, too. They listened without saying a word, until she got to a point in her story where she was on a ship in the ocean, in a storm, conducting research. It was the aspect of research oceanography she loved best: "Figuring out how to adapt to everything that happens while you're at sea and still come back with the data that you needed, and the accuracy that you needed. I loved that challenge," she said. "Then you've got to work up the data and write the papers as sort of penance to be able to go out to sea again the next year."

George Abbey interrupted her just as she was describing how, in the middle of the storm, in the middle of the night, a critical piece of research equipment had busted. She'd had to haul it into the boat in the darkness and inspect each segment. The oceanographer in charge of the expedition had watched her labor for the first few hours but finally turned grumpy. "Just fix the damn thing," he had said, and gone to bed.

"So what did you do?" Abbey asked her.

"What do you mean what did I do?" she said. "We fixed it."

"And then you went to bed?" he asked.

"I felt like saying, *No, you idiot, I did not go to bed.*" Instead she explained that she had stayed up for two more hours, to make sure her fix held in the storm. Later NASA had her take a Myers-Briggs–type personality test. Like virtually all the astronauts—but unlike roughly 85 percent of the American population—she profiled as a "mission-driven" person. "The mission-driven type was overrepresented in the astronaut population," she said. "Whereas more dreamer- or salesman-type folks are very underrepresented."

From the original eight thousand or so applicants, NASA selected thirty-five to become astronauts. Six were women, all scientists. A lot of the men were indeed former fighter pilots. They tended to see themselves as the main event and, at least at first, looked upon the women scientists assigned to accompany them as a sideshow. Kathy wasn't shy about expressing her thoughts on this subject. *You know you're just my taxi driver*, she told one of the pilots. *My job is the interesting part of this mission.* He didn't like it, but the space program was changing. "By the time I got to it," she said, "it had gone from just proving you could get there and come home alive to: what are we doing here?"

What they were doing in space was what she sensed she'd been put on earth to do: explore, gather data, and make sense of it. "The science was three big things," she said. "Bullet point one: using space as a platform to look back at Earth and out into the cosmos. Getting a different point of view. There is a kind of understanding of this planet that space alone makes possible. Bullet point two: What do we need to know that we don't know about living in space? Bullet point three: How does the human body respond to being sprung from the force of gravity? How do fluids flow? How does the body behave?"

What had grabbed her attention from the start was the earth science. The snapshot that might be taken of Earth from above, of the current conditions on Earth that were going to be crucial to mankind's understanding of its environment. "I was all about bullet point one," said Kathy.

She couldn't just skip the other bullet points, however. She might see her job as gathering data about the planet; but a lot of other people saw their jobs as gathering data about *her*. They now had another kind of human body to study, though it was reluctant. ("I was moderately disinterested in being a lab rat.") It didn't help that the engineers at the heart of the space program had some strange notions about women—for instance, that they were more vulnerable to rapid decreases in pressure. "The air force worked with this aerospace medical unit," she said. "They'd concluded that the women were more likely to experience the bends when the pressure went from high to low. They think they've detected a higher instance of damage to the central nervous system. They tell them I'm going to die." She thought: *You guys don't have enough data, and the data you have you've handled badly.* She pointed out that female deep-sea divers didn't experience any special problems at lower depths.

It was an open question as to which was more mysterious to a male NASA engineer: outer space or the American female. They appeared to have better data on outer space. They had prepared makeup kits for their space shuttles, for instance, even though Kathy and a couple of the other women didn't wear makeup. They set out to design flame-retardant one-size-fits-all bras and underpants, until the women explained that the one-size-fits-all approach used for men's underwear wasn't going to work with women's underwear. In the end, the women won the right to buy their own flame-retardant underwear. And how would a woman urinate in space? The engineers worried about that one for a while. The male astronauts had been fitted with condom catheters, but these were always threatening to leak or even burst and obviously wouldn't work for women. To everyone's relief, a NASA engineer created an extra-absorbent polymer and worked it into a diaper that could be worn by all. (In the bargain he'd anticipated the baby diapers of the future.)

And of course, the male engineers were seriously worried about what might ensue if a woman had her period in space. "The idea that women might menstruate in orbit drove the whole place up a wall," said Kathy. "The male world's response was, *Oh, that's ok. We'll just suppress their periods.* We all looked at each other and said, 'You and what other army, buddy?'" The engineers finally agreed to pack tampons in the supply kits. The first time Kathy opened her kit she saw that each tampon had been removed from its paper wrapper and sealed in a plastic fireproof case. Heat-sealed tampons. Each plastic case was connected to another. She pulled on the top one and out pops this great long chain of little red plastic cases, like a string of firecrackers. Hundreds of tampons, for one woman to survive for a few days in space. "It was like a bad stage act," she said. "There just seemed this endless unfurling of Lord only knows how many tampons."

The engineers eventually sat down with the female astronauts to discuss the matter.

"Would one hundred be the right number?" they asked.

Kathy Sullivan worried that NASA might use the differences between their bodies as an excuse "to write different rules for males and females." The male astronauts, on the other hand, adapted pretty quickly to the presence of women. The guy she'd been assigned to walk with in space was named Dave Leestma. They'd had a moment together that captured the spirit of their interaction. They had started training in their space suits. Step 1 was to remove their clothes and put on the first layer of the 225-pound suit—the Liquid Cooling and Ventilation Garment. The test chamber was full of male engineers. "I have this fleeting sense that everyone has just realized that we're about to go boldly where no man has gone before—there's a woman in this mix," said Kathy, in the NASA oral history. "So I looked over at Dave and said, 'Dave, let me tell you my philosophy about modesty in circumstances like this.' He shifts a bit and says, 'Okay.' I said, 'I have none.' He said, 'Fine.' We start peeling off clothes."

Kathy couldn't have been less interested in the gender drama. She just wanted to go to space and "see it for myself, not in a magazine picture." She wanted to get on with the mission. Which was why she never complained about her space suit. "It was a small, medium, large kind of thing—not a custom fit kind of thing," she said. "My knee was never in the knee of the suit. The suits were stiff and took real muscle to move. Whenever I had to bend my legs I had to overcome this extra leverage." By the time she realized that her suit was never going to fit, NASA had asked her to wear it. "I was not going to turn this into 'See, we told you she'd be all this extra trouble.' I decided, 'We're just sucking this up.'" But really, her space suit should have come with a warning label. In a test chamber, a NASA engineer had flipped the switch that enabled the space suit's emergency oxygen tank, and the suit had exploded in a giant fireball. "If you're doing some weird test that's unlike anything that you normally do, it would still get your full attention," Kathy said later, "but this was like saying that when you step on the gas of your car, it's going to explode. Highly discomfiting."

It was now October 11, 1984. The *Challenger* was in orbit, with her inside it, waiting to walk in space. The air was gone from the airlock. When they simulated this moment back on Earth they put a baking pan with water on the floor, to illustrate what might happen to your body's fluids if something went wrong with your suit. As the pressure dropped, the water would bubble violently, as if it were boiling. But then a couple of seconds later it would flash-freeze into ice crystals. Poof. "Don't open your visor!" they said.

On a mission this complicated, it was actually impossible to imagine everything that might kill you. The O-rings of the very spacecraft in whose airlock she now floated would soon become the most famous illustration of the point. Just fifteen months later, the failure of NASA to heed engineers' warnings about how brittle the rings that sealed the solid rocket boosters could become in the cold would lead the boosters to leak and the *Challenger* to blow up, killing all the astronauts on board.

Later, when someone asked her why it never seemed to occur to her to be afraid, Kathy had an answer. In college she'd gone bushwhacking with a boyfriend around the Grand Canyon. They'd hacked a trail in a bad place, and they now had to jump onto a narrow ledge or go tumbling down a steep slope. The slightest misstep and she would fall to her death. "I mean, my knees are wobbling and shaking and I remember thinking: not now." Then she was fine. She'd discovered an emotional talent: she had the ability to decide not to be afraid. All the astronauts had it, she noticed. "If you are scared, I don't want you to be there," she said. "Be *here. Now.* Here. Now. This is the game. Be scared before. Be scared later. Not during."

Inside her space suit, with the pressure gone from the *Challenger*'s airlock, she felt no change at all, and that struck her here as strange, just as it had on Earth. "I always thought, Isn't this room supposed to look different when it has no air in it? But there's no difference!" She moved along a handrail to open the hatch. She poked her head out into space. Then she reached out and tethered herself to the hook on the outside of the capsule, before untethering herself from the hook inside the airlock. "Mountaineering 101." With her body traveling at 17,500 miles per hour she set out, hand over hand, to demonstrate that it was indeed possible to refuel a satellite in orbit. With that, she became the first American woman to walk in space.

That first step would shadow her for the rest of her life. President Reagan would invite her to a dinner at the White House and sit her beside him. Corporations would offer her high-paying jobs. Civic organizations across the country would offer her awards and ask her to come and tell her story. Seemingly all of Long Island would soon be in touch, because at some point in space she had looked down—how could she not—and shouted, "Hey, there's Long Island!" She had a choice of how to play her experience. "You can dine out on this stuff forever," she said, "but that was feeling shallow to me. I wanted to make the experience *matter*."

The same internal process that had led her to decline the role of "girl" made it possible for her to pass on the role of "lady astronaut." She flew twice more into space, orbited Earth a few hundred more times, and then, in the early 1990s, went looking for something else to do. She now had a measure of celebrity and needed to make a decision about how best to use it. She wanted another mission that felt as important as the one she'd just completed. She wanted to do earth science, and she wanted the stakes of the science to be high: that wasn't surprising. What was surprising was where she finally found her mission: the United States Department of Commerce.

Around the same time, DJ Patil also wandered into the Commerce Department, though in truth he didn't know it. Physically, he was sitting at a desk on the campus of the

University of Maryland, pursuing his PhD in mathematics. He'd found a security hole in the U.S. government's computers, and he reached through it to grab what he needed. What he needed was a very specific pile of data. That it, like much of the rest of the government's data, resided in the Department of Commerce he hadn't bothered to figure out.

DJ had come to Maryland from California to study with James Yorke, a professor who had coined the term "chaos theory." The idea was simple: some small, barely noticed event can cascade into huge consequences down the road. (The day your parents met, for instance: what if that hadn't happened?) A lot of the drama in his life DJ traced back to a small, little-noticed event in his early childhood: a tendency to reverse the order of numbers. When you see "16" as "61," you have problems in school. Struggling with his assigned tasks, he diverted himself with unassigned ones. Watching spy movies, he became intrigued with picking locks. He'd pick his way into other kids' lockers, move the stuff around inside, then lock them back up—just to freak them out. Then he learned how to pick people's pockets for fun. He'd take the car keys off some unsuspecting grown-up, move his car, then return the keys to the guy's jacket pocket. In the eighth grade he hacked the English teacher's computer and changed the grades—and never got caught. In ninth grade, a prank gone wrong set an entire hillside in a well-to-do Silicon Valley neighborhood on fire. DJ ended up listening to a cop read him his rights. The landowner agreed not to prosecute if DJ agreed to spend the next few months at hard labor, restoring the hillside. While he was doing that he got himself suspended from his English class for exploding a stink bomb, and a few months after that from math class for . . . at that point it hardly mattered. By the time he graduated from high school—after a merciful school administrator changed an F on his transcript to a C—he wasn't the only one who might look at "DJ" and see "JD."

At De Anza Community College he stumbled into a calculus class and liked it. More than liked it. He realized he had a gift for it. The calculus class was another small life event that wound up having big effects. By the time he arrived in Maryland to pursue his PhD, he was still interested in math, but not so much as he was in what might be done with it, to study a lot of otherwise inexplicable things that happened in life and nature. "I was always in love with the patterns in nature," he said, "and what I needed were the tools to understand them. And for me, math was the most sensible."

All sorts of natural phenomena might be modeled and understood with chaos theory. The collapse of the sardine population off the California coast, for example. Or the bizarre long landslides that occurred in the Mojave Desert, where the rocks ended up inexplicably far from where they'd started, given the slope of their journey. "These long run-out landslides are crazy. The question is: how did the rocks end up so far away?" In theory, the new math might explain it. In practice, there wasn't enough data on the movement of the rocks, or the sardine holocaust, for him or anyone else to study them effectively. The same went for traffic jams, the boom-bust cycles in the wolf and deer populations in the American West, and countless other big events triggered by surprisingly small ones.

Then he happened upon the weather. He'd always been interested in it, but never thought of it as something he might study until he discovered that the U.S. government was sitting on a huge trove of weather data. It resided inside something called the National Oceanic and Atmospheric Administration, which was in turn inside the Department of Commerce—but he didn't have any idea of that yet. He was just roaming around servers within the U.S. government, the sole supplier of the data he needed if he was going to get his PhD. "The only place I could get the data was the weather."

———

Since the end of the Second World War, weather data collection has become one of the greatest illustrations of the possibilities of global collaboration and public-spiritedness. Every day thousands of amateur weather observers report data to their governments, as do a lot of experts aboard commercial planes in the sky and on ships at sea. Every day, twice a day, almost nine hundred weather balloons are released from nine hundred different spots on the globe, ninety-two of them by the U.S. government. A half-dozen countries, including the United States, deploy thousands of buoys to collect weather from the ocean surface. Then there's the data collected by billion-dollar satellites and fancy radar stations—in the United States alone, the

National Weather Service maintains 159 high-resolution Doppler radar sites.

The United States shares its weather data with other countries—just as other countries share their weather data with the United States. But back in 1996, when DJ was hacking the Department of Commerce computer servers, weather data was not generally available to even the most enterprising hacker. "It wasn't open to the public," said DJ, "but it turned out there was a hole." What came through that hole was such a vast trove of information that it overwhelmed the capacity of the computers in the University of Maryland's math department, so DJ hunted for other computers at the university he might use. "You can get historical data and play with it," he said "It was the original idea of the internet. I was *that* guy. I didn't have a supercomputer. So I just had to steal that, too."

He'd start work at eight every night, when no one else was using the computers, and go until seven the next morning. He cobbled together enough storage to hold his borrowed treasure. "That was my academic claim to fame," he said. "That I downloaded the Weather Service's data."

As he looked at the data, a couple of things became apparent. First, that the weather forecasts were improving more dramatically than he'd imagined. No one else was paying much attention to this, but for the first time in history the weatherman was becoming useful. Before the Second World War meteorology had been a bit like medicine in the nineteenth century: the demand for expertise was so relentless that the supply had no choice but to make fraudulent appearances. Right through the 1970s, the weather forecaster would look at the available weather information and, relying heavily on his judgment and personal experience, offer a prediction. His vision typically extended no more than thirty-six hours into the future, and even then it was blurry: *snow will fall somewhere over these three states.* For a very long time the weather had been only theoretically predictable—that is, people had some pretty good ideas about how it might be predicted, without being able actually to predict it.

Around the time DJ began downloading it, the weather data had led to practical progress that shocked even the theoreticians. On March 12, 1993, what became known as the Storm of the Century hit the eastern United States. Its force was incredible: waves in the Gulf of Mexico sank a two-hundred-foot ship. Roofs across southern states collapsed under the weight of the snow. Tornadoes killed dozens of people. Travel ceased along the entire Eastern Seaboard.

But the biggest difference between this storm and those that had come before it was that it had been predicted by a model. Following a segment on *CBS Evening News* about the siege of the Branch Davidian compound in Waco, Texas, Louis Uccellini, a meteorologist with the National Weather Service, had warned of the coming massive threat.

The TV hosts had treated the nation's weatherman with amusement—they ended the story by saying, "The weatherman is usually wrong." But this time he wasn't. The National Weather Service had relied on its forecasting model, with no human laying hands on the results, and it had predicted the location and severity of the storm five *days* before it hit. "It was unheard-of," said Uccellini. "When I started in the 1970s, the idea of predicting extreme events was almost forbidden. How can you see a storm before the storm can be seen? This time, states declared an emergency before the first flake of snow. It was just amazing for us to watch. We sat there wrapping our heads around what we'd done." Six years after the storm, Uccellini described the advances in weather prediction from about the end of World War II as "one of the major intellectual achievements of the twentieth century."

The achievements received surprisingly little attention, perhaps because they were, at least at first, difficult to see. It was not as if one day the weather could not be predicted and the next it could be predicted with perfect accuracy. What was happening was a shift in the odds that the weather forecast was right. It was the difference between an ordinary blackjack player and a blackjack player who was counting the cards. Over time the skill means beating, rather than losing to, the house. But at any given moment it is impossible to detect.

DJ could see that this progress was a big deal. A world-historic event. Here you could see chaos theory dramatized, but in reverse. You could rewind history and consider how things might have come out differently if our ability to predict the weather had been even a tiny bit better, or worse. "The failed hostage rescue in Iran was caused by a sandstorm we didn't see coming," said

DJ. "The Kosovo offensive was so effective because we knew we wouldn't have cloud cover." You could pick almost any extreme weather event and imagine a different outcome for it, if only people had known it was coming. The hurricane that struck Galveston, Texas, back in 1900, before anyone thought to name such storms, had struck without warning and killed so many people that no one ever figured out exactly how many had died. Maybe six thousand or maybe twelve thousand. What their grandchildren would know about the weather might have saved them all.

————

Here was yet another illustration of chaos in life: even slight changes in our ability to predict the weather might have fantastic ripple effects. The weather itself was chaotic. Some slight change in the conditions somewhere on the planet could lead to huge effects elsewhere. The academic meteorologists around DJ knew this; the question was what to do about it. The Department of Meteorology at the University of Maryland, as it happened, had led a new movement in forecasting and spurred the National Weather Service to change its approach to its own models. Before December 1992 the meteorologists had simply plugged the data they had into their forecasting model: wind speeds, barometric pressure, ocean temperatures, and so on. But most of the planet's weather went unobserved: there was no hard data. As a result, many of the model's inputs were just estimates—you didn't actually know the

wind speed or barometric pressure or humidity or anything else at every spot on the planet.

An idea pursued at Maryland and a couple of other
places was to run the weather model over and over, with
different initial weather conditions. Alter the conditions
slightly, in reasonable ways. Vary the wind speed, or barometric pressure at 10,000 feet, or the ocean temperature,
or whatever seemed reasonable to vary. (How you did
this was its own art.) Do it twenty times and you wind
up with twenty different forecasts. A range of forecasts
generated a truer prediction of the weather than a single
forecast, because it captured the uncertainty of each one.
Instead of saying, "Here's where the hurricane is going,"
or "We have no idea where the hurricane is going," you
could say, "We don't know for sure where the hurricane
might go, but we have a cone of probability you can use
to make your decisions."

"Ensemble forecasting," the new technique was called.
It implied that every weather forecast—and not just
hurricanes—should include a cone of uncertainty. (Why
they don't is a great question.) "There's a storm coming
on Saturday" means one thing if all the forecasts in the
ensemble say the storm is coming. It means another if some
of the forecasts say there is no chance of rain on Saturday
and others say that a storm is all but certain. Really, the
weather predictions should reflect this uncertainty. "Why
is the newspaper always giving us a five-day forecast?"
asked DJ. "It should be a two-day forecast sometimes. And
it should be a fourteen-day forecast other times."

By the time DJ discovered the security hole in the government's database, the National Weather Service had taken to ensemble forecasting and was generating a dozen or more forecasts for each day. On some days the forecasts would be largely in agreement: slight changes in the estimates of current weather conditions did not lead to big changes in the future weather. At other times they varied radically. That is, sometimes the weather was highly chaotic and sometimes not. DJ quickly saw that instability was not in any way linked to severity: a Category 5 hurricane might keep on being a Cat 5 hurricane without a whole lot of doubt. Then, other times it wouldn't. "Why in the case of one storm are the forecasts all the same, and in the case of another they are all different?" he asked. Why was the weather sometimes highly predictable and other times less so? Or as DJ put it, "Why does a butterfly flapping its wings in Brazil cause or not cause a tornado in Oklahoma?"

With the government's data he was able to contribute a new idea: that the predictability of the weather might itself be quantified. "We all know the weather is chaotic," he said. "The question is: how chaotic. You should be able to assess when a forecast is likely to go seriously bad, versus when the weather is stable." In the end his thesis created a new statistic: how predictable the weather was at any given moment.

When he defended his thesis, in the summer of 2001, he was surprised by what the U.S. government's data had enabled him to do. "As a grad student you're just like, I hope I have something that doesn't suck. You don't actually expect your stuff to work." He wasn't a meteorologist. Yet he'd found new ways to describe the weather. He'd also found, in himself, a more general interest: in data. What else might it be used to discover?

The relevance of that ambition became a bit clearer after the terrorist attacks of September 11, 2001. "There was a sense that this was, among other things, a failure of data analysis," he said. "If we had known how to distinguish signal from noise we'd have seen it and prevented it. 'Hey, why are all these guys suddenly taking flight lessons?'" The assassins' use of credit cards alone, properly analyzed, would have revealed they were up to no good. "The image of a good network is messy," said DJ. "It's really hard to fake messiness. It's hard to fake being an American with a credit card."

The big question now in DJ's world was: How, using data, do you identify threats to U.S. interests? By this time a young postdoc at Maryland, he attended a talk by a guy who ran something called the Defense Threat Reduction Agency. The agency, inside the U.S. Department of Defense, was charged with defending the country against weapons of mass destruction. It was trying to understand terrorist networks so it might disrupt them. "I hear the talk, and I was like, *Wait a second*," DJ recalled. "The idea that if you push a network a certain way it might collapse. Is the network stable or unstable? It's a lot like the question I was asking about weather forecasts." A terrorist network, like a thunderstorm, might be chaotic. Terrorist networks, along with a lot of other security matters, might be better understood through chaos theory. "If you pull out a node in a terrorist cell, does it collapse? Or the opposite: How do we design our electricity grid so that if you take out a node it does NOT collapse?"

Thinking they would make use of his data skills, he went to work at the Department of Defense, where he expected to look for patterns in terrorist networks. But instead of sticking him at a computer, his new employer shipped him off to a couple of former Soviet republics, to track and understand the stockpiles of biological and chemical weapons left behind by the Russians. "They tell me, 'We need you to go to Uzbekistan and Kazakhstan,' and I'm like, 'I'm a *mathematician*.' That was the first question I asked: 'Why me?' They said, 'Hey, you're a doctor.' And I said, 'I'm not that kind of doctor.' And they said, 'Close enough, you'll figure it out.'" After that, they sent him to Iraq, to help rebuild the school system. All of the work was interesting, and a lot of it useful, but it didn't have much to do with his deep ambition. "People still didn't really appreciate how you can use data to transform," he said.

To his surprise, this was true even of people back home where he had grown up, in Silicon Valley, to which he soon returned. Even there he couldn't get a job doing what he wanted to do with data. "I was just trying to figure out where I could be helpful," he said. "Google passed on me. Yahoo! passed on me." His mom knew someone at eBay and so he finally was hired the undignified way. At eBay he tried, and failed, to persuade his superiors to let him use the data on hand to find new ways to detect fraud.

At length he moved to a new, slow-growing company called LinkedIn, where job seekers posted their CVs and attempted to create their own little networks. His new bosses asked him to be Head of Analytics and Data Product Teams. There, for the first time, he found an audience receptive to his pitch. "The same tools you use to identify where bad guys are, you can do with job skills," he said. "You can show people where skills cluster. Where they might belong in the economy. If you're trained in the army in ordnance disposal, maybe you'd be good at mining." The analytics he'd created at LinkedIn had done exactly that—prodded an army bomb expert to find work setting explosives in mines.

Along with much more: in the space of a few years, the interest in data analysis went from curiosity to fad. The fetish for data overran everything from political campaigns to the management of baseball teams. Inside LinkedIn, DJ presided over an explosion of job titles that described similar tasks: analyst, business analyst, data analyst, research sci. The people in human resources complained to him that the company had too many data-related job titles. The company was about to go public, and they wanted to clean up the organization chart. To that end DJ sat down with his counterpart at Facebook, who was dealing with the same problem. What could they call all these data people? "Data scientist," his Facebook friend suggested. "We weren't trying to create a new field or anything, just trying to get HR off our backs," said DJ. He replaced the job titles for some openings with "data scientist." To his surprise, the number of applicants for the jobs skyrocketed. "Data scientists" were what people wanted to be.

In the fall of 2014 someone from the White House called him. Obama was coming to San Francisco and wanted to meet with him. "He'd seen the power of data in his campaign," said DJ, "and he knew there was a new opportunity to use it to transform the country." When the White House asked him if he wanted to bring his wife to the meeting, DJ figured that Obama was looking for more than a conversation. Inside of eight years he'd gone from being a guy who couldn't get a job in Silicon Valley to being a guy the president of the United States wanted to offer a job he couldn't refuse. When Obama did ask DJ to move to Washington, it was DJ's wife who responded. "How do we know if any of this will be of any use?" she asked. "If your husband is as good as everyone says he is, he'll figure it out," said Obama. Which of course made it even harder for DJ to refuse.

DJ went to Washington. His assignment was to figure out how to make better use of the data created by the U.S. government. His title: Chief Data Scientist of the United States. He'd be the first person to hold the job. He made his first call at the Department of Commerce, to meet with Penny Pritzker, the commerce secretary, and Kathy Sullivan, the head of the National Oceanic and Atmospheric Administration. They were pleased to see him but also a bit taken aback that he had come. "They seemed a little surprised I was there," recalled DJ. "I said, 'I'm the data guy and you're the data agency. This is where a huge amount of the data is.' And they're like, 'Yes, but how did you know?'"

━━━

Nobody understood what it did but, then, like so many United States government agencies, the Department of Commerce is seriously misnamed. It has almost nothing to do with commerce directly and is actually forbidden by law from engaging in business. But it runs the United States Census, the only real picture of who Americans are as a nation. It collects and makes sense of all the country's economic statistics—without which the nation would have very little idea of how it was doing. Through the Patent and Trademark Office it tracks all the country's inventions. It contains an obscure but wildly influential agency called the National Institute of Standards and Technology, stuffed with Nobel laureates, which does everything from setting the standards for construction materials to determining the definition of a "second" and of an "inch." (It's more complicated than you might think.) But of the roughly $9 billion spent each year by the Commerce Department, $5 billion goes to NOAA, and the bulk of that money is spent, one way or another, on figuring out the weather. Each and every day, NOAA collects twice as much data as is contained in the entire book collection of the Library of Congress. "Commerce is one of the most misunderstood jobs in the cabinet, because everyone thinks it works with business," says Rebecca Blank, a former acting commerce secretary in the Obama administration and now chancellor of the University of Wisconsin. "It produces public goods that are of value to business, but that's different. Every secretary who comes in thinks Commerce does trade. But trade is maybe ten percent of what Commerce does— if that." The Department of Commerce should really be called the Department of Information. Or maybe the Department of Data.

Get to Know the U.S. Government had not been high on Donald Trump's to-do list, even after he learned that he'd be running it. On the Monday after the presidential election, the same thing that had happened across the rest of the U.S. government happened inside the Department of Commerce: nothing. Dozens of civil servants sat all day waiting to deliver briefings that would, in the end, never be heard. They'd expected Trump's campaign organization to send in Landing Teams to learn about what was being done there, and why. The problems that had been Obama's problems for the past eight years were about to become Trump's problems. But his people didn't seem to want to know about them. "They just didn't bring any bodies in at all," says a senior Commerce official. "There was just very little attention paid to any of the pieces. The Census—they just didn't seem interested in knowing any of that. It all seemed to be about trade. Or the size of the Commerce workforce."

Right up until early January, no one turned up at NOAA to figure out who should run the place and how they would run it. But at the end of November Trump nominated Wilbur Ross, a seventy-nine-year-old Wall Street billionaire, to be the next secretary of commerce. A few weeks later Ross came in for a single meeting with Penny Pritzker. "He came by himself," recalled one of the people who greeted him. "I was shocked. Just this very old guy, all by himself. And it was pretty clear he had no idea what he was getting into. And he had no help."

He also soon had a problem: two billion or so missing dollars. A *Forbes* reporter named Dan Alexander, studying the financial disclosure forms Ross had been required to file with the Office of Government Ethics, had been struck by the discrepancy between how much money Ross said he had, and how much he'd told *Forbes* reporters that he had, over the course of many years. *How had $3.7 billion suddenly become $700 million?* Three point seven billion is what Ross had told *Forbes* he was worth. He'd sent *Forbes* a list of his assets every year for the past thirteen years, so that he would qualify for the magazine's annual list of the four hundred richest Americans. He'd always failed to answer *Forbes*'s follow-up questions, and so the people at *Forbes* who compiled the list reduced the number to $2.9 billion. To be conservative about it.

Alexander was now one of the *Forbes* staffers who compiled the magazine's rich list—and he had access to the *Forbes* files. "I thought this was kind of odd," he said. "It bugged me that it didn't add up. I called Ross up to see what he had to say about it. And he sounds like a credible guy." Ross claimed the explanation was simple: between the election and the inauguration he had simply *given away* two billion dollars to a trust, owned by his heirs.

Alexander had first assumed that the scandal was that Wilbur Ross was hiding money from the U.S. government. But after pressing the Department of Commerce to fill in the giant holes in Ross's story, he realized that Ross had misled *Forbes*. For thirteen years. "I went back in the files," said Alexander. "We [at *Forbes*] had [initially] counted the money that belonged to his investors in one of his funds as his own money. I was stunned that anyone had let that slide. He lucked into a way to be on the list, without deserving to be on the list. But once he gets on the list, he lies. For years." The *Forbes* reporters were accustomed to having rich people mislead them about the size of their wealth, but nearly all of them had been trying to keep their names *off* the list. "In the history of the magazine only three people stand out as having made huge efforts to get on, or end up higher than they belonged," said Alexander. "One was [Saudi] Prince Alwaleed. The second was Donald Trump. And the third was Wilbur Ross."

The scandal wasn't that Wilbur Ross was hiding two billion dollars from the government, but that he'd never had the two billion dollars in the first place. Alexander wrote up his findings, after which, he says, "I got a bunch of calls from people who had worked with or for Wilbur Ross, to say how happy they were the truth finally came out." The former number-three man at Ross's old firm, who had worked with Ross for twenty-five years, spoke on the record. "Wilbur doesn't have an issue with bending the truth," he said. This was the man Trump had chosen to guard the integrity of the data on which our society rests.

Yet inside the Department of Commerce there came, in the spring of 2017, a ray of hope. In March the Trump White House asked the help of a former senior climate policy adviser from the George W. Bush administration who had actually worked for eight years inside the Department of Commerce. "They came into the Department of Commerce," said the former Bush official, "and they discovered that it has got this thing in it called NOAA. And it's sixty percent of the Commerce Department budget. And they said, 'What the fuck is NOAA?'"

The Bush official flew to Washington, DC, to speak with Wilbur Ross about the place Ross was meant to have been running for the past several months. *It's not the Department of Commerce,* the Bush official told him in so many words. *It's the Department of Science and Technology.* It was a massive data-collecting enterprise, and the biggest collector of all was the National Weather Service. NOAA also regulated the fishing industry and mapped the ocean floor and maintained the fleet of ships and planes used in gathering information. It had collected climate and weather data going back to records kept at Monticello by Thomas Jefferson. Without that data, and the Weather Service that made sense of it, no plane would fly, no bridge would be built, and no war would be fought—at least not well. The weather data was also the climate data. "If you don't believe in climate change, you at least want to understand the climate," said the Bush official. And if you wanted to understand the climate, you needed to take special care of NOAA's data.

There was no way the Bush official could get across all he wanted to tell the new commerce secretary in a single meeting. "NOAA is a beast," he said. "It's twelve thousand employees and they are decentralized—out in these little tiny offices all over the country. But it does more to protect Americans than any other agency except for Homeland Security and the Department of Defense." The Bush official did get to tell Ross his main point about NOAA. "It's incredible value and everyone shits on it," he said. "The people are great. They aren't in it for the money. They're in it for the mission." And he asked Ross a question: "What's your philosophy for running the department?"

"What do you mean?" asked Ross.

"It's not really the Department of Commerce," said the Bush official. "Its mission is a science and technology mission."

"Yeah, I don't think I want to be focusing on that," said Ross.

"It was clear to me that he had not thought about what the science and technology meant," said the Bush official. "He doesn't have a scientific bone in his body."

That was totally okay. The secretary of commerce could continue to pretend to be the Secretary of Business. But he badly needed to put people in place under him who understood the science. The Bush official assumed he'd been brought in for just this reason: to help the new administration find the right person to run NOAA. He knew qualified Republicans, inoffensive to Trump. He handed the Trump White House a list of half a dozen politically acceptable people who could do the job well enough.

Six months later, in October 2017, the White House announced its selection: Barry Myers.

———

Barry Myers hadn't been anywhere near the Bush official's list. He was the CEO of AccuWeather, one of the first for-profit weather companies. It had been founded by his meteorologist brother, Joel Myers, back in 1962. A third brother helped to run the company, which employed other family members, including Barry Myers's wife, Holly. The company was still privately owned by the Myers family, so it was hard to know exactly how big it was, or how much money it made, or how it made it. Staffers in the U.S. Senate charged with vetting Myers's nomination estimated that AccuWeather had roughly $100 million a year in revenue, and that it came mainly from selling ads on its website and selling weather forecasts to companies and governments willing to pay for them. Some weather geeks had recently discovered that the company had been selling the locations of people using its app, even when these individuals had declined to give AccuWeather permission to do this. At any rate, at his U.S. Senate hearings, Barry Myers estimated his AccuWeather shares to be worth roughly $57 million.

At first glance, the nomination made sense: a person deeply involved in weather forecasting was going to take over an agency that devoted most of its resources to understanding the weather. At second glance, both Barry Myers and AccuWeather were deeply inappropriate. For a start, Barry Myers wasn't a meteorologist or a scientist of any sort. He was a lawyer. "I was originally enrolled in meteorology as an undergraduate," he told the *Wall Street Journal* back in 2014. "I then dropped out of school because I was a horrible student. I was never interested in learning, which I look at now as sort of funny."

Then there was AccuWeather. It had started out making its money by repackaging and selling National Weather Service information to gas companies and ski resorts. It claimed to be better than the National Weather Service at forecasting the weather, but what set it apart from everyone else was not so much its ability to predict the weather as to market it. As the private weather industry grew, AccuWeather's attempts to distinguish itself from its competitors became more outlandish. In 2013, for instance, it began to issue a forty-five-day weather forecast. In 2016 that became a ninety-day weather forecast. "We are in the realm of palm reading and horoscopes here, not science," Dan Satterfield, a meteorologist on CBS's Maryland affiliate, wrote. "This kind of thing should be condemned, and if you have an AccuWeather app on your smartphone, my advice is to stand up for science and replace it."

Alone in the private weather industry, AccuWeather made a point of claiming that it had "called" storms missed by the National Weather Service. Here was a typical press release: "*On the evening of Feb. 24, 2018, several tornadoes swept across northern portions of the Lower Mississippi Valley*

*causing widespread damage, injuries and unfortunately some fatal-
ities. . . . AccuWeather clients received pinpointed SkyGuard®
Warnings, providing them actionable information and more lead
time than what was given by the government's weather service in
issuing public warnings and other weather providers who rely on
government warnings . . ."*

All AccuWeather's press releases shared a couple of problems: 1) there was no easy way to confirm them, as the
forecasts were private, and the clients unnamed; and 2)
even if true they didn't mean very much. A company selling private tornado warnings can choose the predictions
on which it is judged. When it outperforms the National
Weather Service, it issues a press release bragging about
its prowess. When it is outperformed by the National
Weather Service it can lay low. But it is bound to be better
at least every now and again: the dumb blackjack player is
sometimes going to beat the card counter. "You have these
anecdotes [from AccuWeather], but there is no data that
says they are fundamentally improving on the National
Weather Service tornado forecasts," says David Kenny,
chief executive of the Weather Company, a subsidiary of
IBM, which, among other things, forecasts turbulence for
most of the U.S. commercial airline industry.

The closest thing to an authority on the relative accuracy of various weather forecasts is a website called Fore-
castAdvisor. It began, as so much weather research seems
to, almost by accident. Its founder, Eric Floehr, was managing a team of software developers and went looking for
material on which to practice a new programming lan-

guage. He stumbled upon weather forecasts—and a funny situation. All the forecasters were claiming to be better than each other: they couldn't all be right. "When I started in 2003, the private weather companies—AccuWeather, for example—are saying, 'We're the Number 1 forecast!' So I called them and said, 'You make this claim that you are the most accurate forecast: what are you basing it on?' They faxed me back an undergraduate paper written for a science fair that looked at forecasts for three months of one summer in Washington, DC. That was the best data they had to make that claim."

Over the next thirteen years, Floehr collected eight hundred million weather forecasts. "I was curious. Was there really a difference? *I live in Paducah, Kentucky. Should I look at AccuWeather or the Weather Channel?*'" Lo and behold, there really was a difference. In the seemingly simple matter of predicting the high temperature for the day, some forecasters were better than others. None of them was consistently better all the time, however. Some were more accurate in some parts of the country than they were in others. Some were more accurate in some months of the year than in others. And there was no answering the question of who was better at tornado alerts or hurricane-track predictions or flood warnings, or at calling other life-threatening weather, because the private companies did not reveal their predictions of those events to anyone but their paying customers.

So Floehr analyzed everyone's ability to predict the high temperature on any given day. From 2003 up until 2011, the National Weather Service's forecasts had been as good as the most accurate private weather forecast, including AccuWeather's. Since 2011, the private weather forecasters have been slightly more accurate than the National Weather Service. Still, says Floehr, "For sure I'm going to listen to the National Weather Service when they issue a tornado warning or a flash flood warning. I'm not going to trust right now AccuWeather or the Weather Channel."

Floehr's analysis uncovered two big trends in weather prediction. One was toward greater relative accuracy in the private sector—which of course was totally dependent on the National Weather Service data for its forecasts. The other was the astonishing improvement in all weather predictions. The five-day-out forecast in 2016 was as accurate as the one-day-out forecast had been in 2005. In just the last few years, for the first time in history, a meteorologist's forecast of how hot it will be nine days from now is better than just guessing.

Barry Myers liked to say that he was in competition with the federal government. If so, the competition was bizarre: the U.S. Department of Commerce gave him, for free, most of the raw material he needed to create his product. Without the weather satellites, weather radar, weather buoys, and weather balloons, there would be no weather forecasting worth listening to, much less paying for. Whatever AccuWeather—and any other private weather forecaster—might be doing to refine the National Weather Service's forecasts also depended on having those forecasts in the first place. "If the Weather Service forecast wasn't there, all the private weather forecasts would get worse," says David Kenny.

But the National Weather Service was forbidden by law from advertising the value of its services—and if it even hinted at doing so, Barry Myers could apply pressure on it in all manner of ways. AccuWeather might make any sort of wild boast it wanted to about the accuracy of its weather prediction. It might disparage the very people who supplied it with the information it had used to make that prediction. The meteorologists at the National Weather Service had no real ability or even inclination to respond. "We had to drag them kicking and screaming into defending themselves against false charges," says a former Obama Commerce Department official. "They never claim credit. They always do these intensely self-critical how-can-we-do-better inquiries. It's a public safety mentality: they do what they do because they really sincerely and since they were eight years old love the science and the service, not because they care at all about credit or glory."

That was the sad truth—the public servants couldn't or wouldn't defend themselves, and few outside the U.S. government had a deep interest in sticking up for them. By the 1990s, Barry Myers was arguing with a straight face that the National Weather Service should be, with one exception, entirely forbidden from delivering any weather-related knowledge to any American who might otherwise wind up a paying customer of AccuWeather. The exception was when human life and property was at stake. Even here Myers hedged. "The National Weather Service does not need to have the final say on warnings," he told the consulting firm McKinsey, which made a study of the strangely fraught relationship between the private weather sector and the government. "The customer and the private sector should be able to sort that out. The government should get out of the forecasting business."

In 2005 Rick Santorum, a senator from AccuWeather's home state of Pennsylvania and a recipient of Myers family campaign contributions, introduced a bill that would have written this idea into law. The bill was a little vague, but it appeared to eliminate the National Weather Service's website or any other means of communication with the public. It allowed the Weather Service to warn people about the weather just before it was about to kill them, but at no other time—and exactly how anyone would be any good at predicting extreme weather if he or she wasn't predicting all the other weather was left unclear.

Pause a moment to consider the audacity of that maneuver. A private company whose weather predictions were totally dependent on the billions of dollars spent by the U.S. taxpayer to gather the data necessary for those predictions, and on decades of intellectual weather work sponsored by the U.S. taxpayer, and on international data-sharing treaties made on behalf of the U.S. taxpayer, and on the very forecasts that the National Weather Service generated, was, in effect, trying to force the U.S. taxpayer to pay all over again for what the National Weather Service might be able to tell him or her for free.

After Santorum's bill failed to pass, AccuWeather's strategy appeared, to those inside the Weather Service, to change. Myers spent more time interacting directly with the Weather Service. He got himself appointed to various NOAA advisory boards. He gave an AccuWeather board seat to Conrad Lautenbacher, who had run NOAA in the second Bush administration. He became an insistent presence in the lives of the people who ran the Weather Service. And wherever he saw them doing something that might threaten his profits, he jumped in to stop it. After the Joplin tornado, the Weather Service set out to build an app, to better disseminate warnings to the public. AccuWeather already had a weather app, Myers barked, and the government should not compete with it. ("Barry Myers is the reason we don't have the app," says a senior National Weather Service official.) In 2015, the Weather Company offered to help NOAA put its satellite data in the cloud, on servers owned by Google and Amazon. Virtually all the satellite data that came into NOAA wound up in places where no one could ever see it again. The Weather Company simply sought to render it accessible to the public. Myers threatened to sue the Weather Service if they did it. "He stopped it," said David Kenny. "We were willing to donate the technology to NOAA for free. We just wanted to do a science project to prove that we could."

Myers claimed that, by donating its time and technology to the U.S. government, the Weather Company might somehow gain a commercial advantage. The real threat to AccuWeather here was that many more people would have access to weather data. "It would have been a leap forward for all the people who had the computing power to do forecasts," said Kenny. One senior official at the Department of Commerce at the time was struck by how far this one company in the private sector had intruded into what was, in the end, a matter of public safety. "You're essentially taking a public good that's been paid for with taxpayer dollars and restricting it to the privileged few who want to make money off it," he said.

By early 2018 Barry Myers had, by some mysterious process, gotten himself one Senate floor vote away from running NOAA. How he went about trying to secure that vote was deeply disturbing, at least in the eyes of the U.S. Senate staffers vetting his nomination. "We don't hear much from the White House," said one. "But the Accu-Weather lobbyist is up here all the time. It's almost like it [NOAA] has been subcontracted to him, which is bizarre. It's Trump saying, 'If it is worth it to you, go get it.' Normally the White House would be doing this." Myers, for his part, was evasive. During the confirmation process, he was asked to name the people who sat on the AccuWeather board. Myers declined; the information belonged to the company and wasn't his own to disclose, he indicated. But just a short time earlier, in a private meeting, he had rattled the names off easily. (Several of them were members of his family.) He claimed he would sell his stake in AccuWeather but did not explain how or to whom. "He says he's going to sell his AccuWeather shares, but he could sell it to his brother for a dollar and buy it back for a dollar when he leaves office," says Walter Shaub, former head of the Office of Government Ethics.

In his bizarre competition with the National Weather Service, there were two ways for Barry Myers to win. His family business might consistently make better weather forecasts and earn the trust of paying customers through its virtuosity. Or it could make the National Weather Service forecasts worse—or at least less accessible. As a private citizen Myers devoted considerable energy to making the National Weather Service *seem* worse. As a public servant he could do much more. "Barry is uniquely dangerous, in a way a Scott Pruitt is not," said a Senate staffer. "Scott Pruitt does not understand the agency [Environmental Protection] he's trying to destroy. Barry's skills make him more effective in dismantling NOAA. There are a million little things he could do that we will never understand."

Another McKinsey study estimated that the entire industry generated somewhere between $2 billion and $4 billion a year in revenue and was growing fast. With reason. The annual cost of natural disasters in the 1980s had been $50 billion. Hurricane Sandy alone inflicted over $65 billion worth of damage. The private weather industry, unlike the National Weather Service, has a financial interest in catastrophe. The more spectacular and expensive the disasters, the more people will pay for warning of them. The more people stand to lose, the more money they will be inclined to pay. The more they pay, the more the weather industry can afford to donate to elected officials, and the more influence it will gain over the political process.

The dystopic endgame is not difficult to predict: the day you get only the weather forecast you pay for. A private company will become better than the Weather Service at knowing where a hurricane will make landfall: What will it do with that information? Tell the public or trade it inside a hedge fund? You know what Hurricane Harvey is going to do to Houston before Houston knows: Do you help Houston? Or do you find clever ways to make money off Houston's destruction?

One version of the future revealed itself in March 2015. The National Weather Service had failed to spot a tornado before it struck Moore, Oklahoma. It had spun up and vanished very quickly, but, still, the people in the Weather Service should have spotted it. AccuWeather quickly issued a press release bragging that it had sent a tornado alert to its paying corporate customers in Moore twelve minutes before the tornado hit. The big point is that AccuWeather never broadcast its tornado warning. The only people who received it were the people who had paid for it—and God help those who hadn't. While the tornado was touching down in Moore, AccuWeather's network channel was broadcasting videos of . . . hippos, swimming.

When, at the request of the Trump White House, the former Bush Commerce Department official wrote up his list of people he believed were suited to run the National Oceanic and Atmospheric Administration, and the National Weather Service inside it, it never occurred to him to put Barry Myers's name on it. "I don't want someone who has a bottom line, or a concern with shareholders, in charge of saving lives and protecting property," he said. But it was more than that. To put Barry Myers in charge of NOAA was to give him control over maybe the most valuable and necessary pile of data that the U.S. government collects. "The more people have access to the weather data, the better it is for the country," said the Bush official. "There's *so* much gold in there. People just don't know how to get to it."

—————

DJ Patil had gone to Washington in 2014 to help people find that gold. He was the human expression of an executive order Obama had signed the year before, insisting that all unclassified government data be made publicly available and that it be machine-readable. DJ assumed he'd need to leave when the man who hired him left office, so that gave him just two years. "We did not have time to collect new data," he said. "We were just trying to open up what we had."

He set out to make as many connections as possible between the information and the people who could make new sense of it—to encourage them to use the data in novel and interesting ways. "I was looking to find people like me, when I was a student," he said. "We're going to open all the data and go to every economics department and say, 'Hey, you want a PhD?' In every agency there were questions to be answered. Most of the answers we have gotten have not come from government. They've come from the broad American public who has access to the data."

The opioid crisis was a case in point. The data scientists in the Department of Health and Human Services had opened up the Medicaid and Medicare data, which held information about prescription drugs. Journalists at ProPublica had combed through it and discovered odd concentrations of opioid prescriptions. "We would never have figured out that there *was* an opioid crisis without the data," said DJ.

The big pools of raw facts accumulated by the federal government are windows into American life. A team of researchers at Stanford University, led by an economist named Raj Chetty, used newly accessible data from the Internal Revenue Service to write a series of papers that addressed questions of opportunity in American life. One, titled "The Fading American Dream," asked a simple question: How likely is it that an American child will be better off than his parents? The IRS data allowed Chetty to study Americans across generations, and the census data let him compare them by race, gender, or whichever trait he wished to isolate. In the data he found an answer to his question, and much more. He discovered that while just over 90 percent of children born in 1940 went on to earn more than their parents, only 50 percent of children born in the 1980s did so. Every year, the economic future of an American child was a bit less bright. And the big reason was not lower rates of economic growth but the increasingly unequal distribution of money. More and more of the gains were being captured by the very rich. Mobility had a racial dimension as well: A white child born into the upper-income quintile was five times more likely to stay there than to fall to the bottom. A black child born into the upper-income quintile was as likely to fall to the bottom as to remain rich.

More of America's problems than even DJ had imagined could be better understood and addressed with better access to the right information. The problem of excessive police force was another example. After a white policeman shot a defenseless black man in Ferguson, Missouri, the White House convened police chiefs from ten American cities, along with their data. The policing data was local and difficult to get ahold of—and that was DJ's point. He wanted to show what might be possible if the government collected the information. "We asked the question: What causes excessive use of police force?" Combing the data from the ten cities, a team of researchers from several American universities found a pattern that would have been hard to spot with the naked eye. Police officers who had just come from an emotionally fraught situation—a suicide, or a domestic abuse call in which a child was involved—were more likely to use excessive force. Maybe the problem wasn't as simple as a bad cop. Maybe it was the emotional state in which the cop had found himself. "Dispatch sent them right back out without time to decompress," said DJ. "Give them a break in between and maybe they behave differently."

A young guy in the White House pulled up stop-and-search rates from another pile of policing data. He discovered that a black person in a car was no more likely to be pulled over by the police than a white person. The difference was what happened next. "If you're black you're way more likely to get searched," said DJ. But then he noticed another pattern: not all the cops exhibited the same degree of racial bias. A few cops in one southern city were *ten times* more likely than others to search a black person they had pulled over. Right there in the White House, the young researcher showed the data to the city's police chief. "He genuinely had no idea," said DJ. "He was like, 'Can you please tell me more?'"

In the end, even DJ Patil was shocked by the possibilities that lurked in the raw piles of information the government had acquired. "I didn't grasp the scope at first," he said. And if you wanted to see the possibilities—the value that the entire society might reap from letting smart people loose on the data—you needed to look no further than David Friedberg.

———

In 2006 Friedberg was driving home in the rain to San Francisco from his job in Mountain View when he noticed how differently people behaved when it rained. The weather affected all sorts of businesses, though not so much Google, where Friedberg worked. The specific business that had caught Friedberg's eye was a bike rental company near Bayside Village on the Embarcadero. When it rained, no one rented bikes.

Obviously.

Friedberg had graduated from the University of California–Berkeley five years earlier, with a degree in astrophysics. He was twenty-seven years old but could pass for sixteen. Because of where he lived and who he worked for, it was second nature for him to think, *If I can get my hands on data and quantify weather risk, I can sell weather insurance to the businesses that need it.* Ski resorts, airlines, utility companies, golf courses, packagers of beach vacations— there was really no end of industries, or even governments, that he might serve. Every inch of snow cost the City of New York $1.8 million dollars.

He found a few friends and angel investors to back him and hired a group of mathematicians to collect and analyze weather data. "Math people figure shit out," he said. His math people soon discovered the rich haul of weather data inside the Department of Commerce. They asked for and received the historical rainfall and temperature data from the National Weather Service's two hundred weather stations. They discovered that NOAA had collected, for the previous forty years, rainfall and temperature at every American airport, however small. They learned that NOAA maintained 158 radar installations, and that these recorded a big percentage of the rain that had fallen in America during the past fifty years—along with anything else that happened to be in the air. That's how the United States government had found the pieces of the *Columbia* after the space shuttle exploded in midair: using NOAA's radar.

The federal government has the sort of data on the weather that the Boston Red Sox has on Major League Baseball players. But unlike the Red Sox, it had made little effort to exploit the value in it. The images from the radar stations, for instance. They were on tapes in a basement of a NOAA office in Asheville, North Carolina. To get the data into a form he could use, Friedberg paid NOAA to put it on hard drives and ship them to him. He then moved the data, for free, to the cloud. "That was the first data set we were able to get onto the cloud," said Ed Kearns, chief data officer at NOAA. "David showed Google and Amazon and Microsoft that there was a business case for taking it. Until we got it up, no one was able to reprocess the data."

Of course, without cloud computing there would have been no place to put the radar data. But once it was on the cloud it was generally accessible and could be used for any purpose. (Ornithologists at Cornell University would soon be using it to study bird migrations.) The math team at Friedberg's new company, which he called WeatherBill, used it to calculate the weather odds for some very specific situations. "What is risk?" asked Friedberg. "Risk is uncertainty about the outcome. The less data you have, the more uncertainty you have about the outcome." If you are the first person to cross the ocean on a ship, you are going to have trouble insuring yourself. If you are the thousandth ship, there is now data that certain kinds of ships do better than others, certain times of year are more treacherous than others, certain kinds of hulls are more durable, and so forth. "The more data we captured, the more we were able to determine the probabilities of some unfortunate event occurring," said Friedberg. "But there were private companies, like AccuWeather and the Weather Company, that had issues with us getting access to weather data. In the end we agreed [with NOAA] we would not have access to the weather data *today*. We'd just get the historical data."

It took eighteen months before WeatherBill had a website on which anyone could come and insure himself against the weather. And people did turn up, in fits and spurts. The U.S. Open tennis tournament bought rain insurance, for example, as did the broadcaster that aired the matches. "Anything more than 0.01 inches of rain per hour means they can't play that hour," said Friedberg. Other interested parties included an Arizona ski resort, a pair of golf courses, a beach resort in Barbados, a car wash, and a hummus shop called Hummus Brothers. Friedberg hadn't known that people bought less hummus when it rained but, then, he was learning all sorts of odd stuff about people's exposure to the weather. Salad places did much better on sunny days; coffee shops did not.

But Friedberg also learned that it was harder to sell weather insurance than he had supposed. "He had this quaint supposition that there were all of these people looking for this online," says one of his former business partners. "And they weren't."

By 2008 Friedberg realized that if he wanted to meet the people who needed weather insurance, he'd have to hit the road and find them. That's when he stumbled on the California citrus packers. The year before, in 2007, there'd been a bad freeze. The citrus farmers were able to obtain some insurance through the federal government, but the companies that packed and shipped the fruit were not. "If the temperature goes below 28 degrees for four hours or more, they have no business," said Friedberg. The California citrus packers had learned that the hard way. "Then we started talking to the growers," said Friedberg, "and they weren't fully covered, either. And we thought: if this is just citrus, agriculture must be big."

That was the turning point for David Friedberg. He realized that the people most exposed to the weather and most receptive to insuring themselves against it were farmers. The *Farmers' Almanac* had offered them weather predictions for the growing season since 1792, but those predictions had never been any better than guessing. The U.S. Department of Agriculture offered insurance against catastrophic crop loss but still left farmers with lots of exposure. There was a need. There was also a problem: to evaluate the weather risk to any one farmer's crop, Friedberg would need to predict not just the weather but how any given field responded to it. What kind of soil did it have? How well did it retain water? The question became: Where might he find this kind of data?

Once again, the U.S. government had it. NOAA had forty years' worth of infrared satellite images of all the land in the United States—again on tape drives in some basement. Plants absorb visible light and emit infrared light: you could calculate the biomass in a field by how much infrared light it emitted. Friedberg brokered a deal with Google, which had digitized the information and gave him access to it for free. "That's when we discovered that farmers were lying about the dates they were planting," said Friedberg. The federal crop insurance program, seeking to minimize the risk of freeze, stipulated the earliest date that a farmer was allowed to plant. But the earlier the seeds went into the ground, the richer the crop. To qualify for the insurance, farmers had been claiming to have planted their seeds later than they had. The lie had been captured for decades by satellite, but no one had been able to see the data.

Inside the Department of Agriculture, Friedberg's math team found data on the size and shape of every one of America's twenty-six million fields. Inside the Department of the Interior, they found data on the soil composition of those fields. "They said, 'No one has ever asked us for this,'" said Friedberg. That one database was so big that it couldn't be transmitted over the internet. He'd had to pay the government agency to send it on hard drives, which he then sent to engineers at Amazon, who moved it all to the cloud. In each of the six years from 2007 to 2013, Friedberg's company used *forty times* more data than the year before. "All this data, it would never have existed if not for the government infrastructure that collected it," said Friedberg. "There's no private institution that on their own would have collected it. And without it we couldn't have made predictions. We would never have had a business without that data. But by the time we were done, we could really quantify the effects of weather on farming."

In 2011 Friedberg decided to sell exclusively to farmers, and WeatherBill changed its name to The Climate Corporation. "We needed to feel a little less Silicon Valley and less whimsical," said Friedberg. For the next few years he would spend half his time on the road, explaining himself to people whose first step was toward mistrust. "Farmers don't believe anything," he said. "There's always been some bullshit product for farmers. And the people selling it are usually from out of town."

He'd sit down in some barn or wood shop, pull out his iPad, and open up a map of whatever Corn Belt state he happened to be in. He'd let the farmer click on his field. Up popped the odds of various unpleasant weather events—a freeze, a drought, a hailstorm—and his crops' sensitivity to them. He'd show the farmer how much money he would have made in each of the previous thirty years if he had bought weather insurance. Then David Friedberg, Silicon Valley kid, would teach the farmer about his own fields. He'd show the farmer exactly how much moisture the field contained at any given moment—above a certain level, the field would be damaged if worked on. He'd show him the rainfall and temperature every day—which you might think the farmer would know, but then the farmer might be managing twenty or thirty different fields, spread over several counties. He'd show the farmer the precise stage of growth of his crop, the best moments to fertilize, the optimum eight-day window to plant his seeds, and the ideal harvest date.

The fertilizer was a big deal to them. "The biggest expense farmers have is fertilizer," said Friedberg. "They'll spend a hundred bucks an acre on corn seed and two hundred bucks on fertilizer. And their net profit might be a hundred bucks an acre. If it rains right after you fertilize, the fertilizer washes away. So how do you decide when to plant and when to fertilize? I had guys come up to me after and say, 'You saved me four hundred grand last year.'"

Farming had always involved judgment calls that turned on the instincts of the farmer. The Climate Corporation had turned farming into decision science, and a matter of probabilities. The farmer was no longer playing roulette but blackjack. And David Friedberg was helping him to count the cards. "For a lot of these guys it was like, 'My mind is blown,'" Friedberg recalled. "They didn't believe that the knowledge could be created. All the new technology they had ever seen in their lives was physical. New machines, new seeds, new kinds of fertilizer. All these had just been tools for the farmer to use. None of them had replaced the farmer." No one ever asked Friedberg the question: If my knowledge is no longer useful, who needs me? But it was a good question. "There is stuff the farmer picks up on that we haven't got data on yet," he said. "For example, are there bugs in the field? But over time that'll go to zero. Everything will be observed. Everything will be predicted."

About a year after they started selling insurance to farmers, the people at the Climate Corporation noticed something funny was going on. The farmers buying their weather insurance were spending a lot of time playing with the software to which the insurance gave them access. "We found the farmers logging in just to see the data on their fields," said Friedberg. To insure American farm-land, he'd needed to understand the fields better than the farmers did themselves: now they knew it. "We thought we were in the insurance business, but we were actually in the knowledge business," said Friedberg. "It went from being insurance to being recommendations for farmers." That first year, in 2011, the Climate Corporation gener-ated $60 million in sales, just from selling weather insur-ance to farmers. Three years later they were insuring 150 million acres of American farmland—the bulk of the Corn Belt—and teaching the farmers how to farm them more efficiently. Six years after venture capitalists valued David Friedberg's new company at $6 million, Monsanto bought it for $1.1 billion.

And yet through the entire experience, David Friedberg had this growing sense of unease. "When you come from San Francisco and grew up in Silicon Valley, every mea-sure is about progress," he said. "The progress in society. The progress in the economy. The progress of technology. And you kind of get used to that. And you think that's the norm in the way the world operates, because you see everything getting better. Then you get on a plane and if you land anywhere but a big city, it feels the same. It's total stagnation. It's 'we've been farming the same six fields for the last seventy years.' It's getting married at nineteen or twenty. It's the opposite of progression. Life is about keep-ing up. Life is about keeping everything the same."

People in the places he'd traveled lived from paycheck to paycheck. They were exposed to risks in ways that he was not: the weather was just one of those risks. He began to notice other kinds of data—for instance, that 40 percent of Americans can't cover an unexpected expense of a thousand bucks. The farmers usually weren't so bad off, but their situation was inherently precarious and threatened by modernity. Farmers didn't work on desktop computers, and so they'd largely skipped the initial internet revolution. But they had mobile phones, and in 2008, when the 3G networks went up in rural America, farmers finally got online. "The problem with the internet is that it shows everyone on earth what they're missing," said Friedberg. "And if you can't get to it, you feel you are getting fucked. That there is this very visceral and obvious shift that is happening in the world that you're missing out on."

At the same time David Friedberg was helping farmers to secure their immediate economic future, he was threatening their identity. *Your family has been tilling this same soil for a century, and yet this data-crunching machine I've built in just a few years can do it better.* The phrase was a whisper underlying every conversation he'd had with a farmer.

Friedberg played in a high-stakes poker game with some friends in the tech world. In their last game before the 2016 presidential election, he offered to bet anyone who would take the other side that Donald Trump would win.

═══════

After Trump took office, DJ Patil watched with wonder as the data disappeared across the federal government. Both the Environmental Protection Agency and the Department of the Interior removed from their websites the links to climate change data. The USDA removed the inspection reports of businesses accused of animal abuse by the government. The new acting head of the Consumer Financial Protection Bureau, Mick Mulvaney, said he wanted to end public access to records of consumer complaints against financial institutions. Two weeks after Hurricane Maria, statistics that detailed access to drinking water and electricity in Puerto Rico were deleted from the FEMA website. In a piece for FiveThirtyEight, Clare Malone and Jeff Asher pointed out that the first annual crime report released by the FBI under Trump was missing nearly three-quarters of the data tables from the previous year. "Among the data missing from the 2016 report is information on arrests, the circumstances of homicides (such as the relationships between victims and perpetrators), and the only national estimate of annual gang murders," they wrote. Trump said he wanted to focus on violent crime, and yet was removing the most powerful tool for understanding it.

And as for the country's first chief data scientist—well, the Trump administration did not show the slightest interest in him. "I basically knew that these guys weren't going to listen to us," said DJ, "so we created these exit memos. The memos showed that this stuff pays for itself a thousand times over." He hoped the memos might give the incoming administration a sense of just how much was left to be discovered in the information the government had collected. There were questions crying out for answers: for instance, what was causing the boom in traffic fatalities? The Department of Transportation had giant pools of data waiting to be searched. One hundred Americans were dying every day in car crashes. The thirty-year trend of declining traffic deaths has reversed itself dramatically. "We don't really know what's going on," said DJ. "Distracted driving? Heavier cars? Faster driving? More driving? Bike lanes?"

The knowledge to be discovered in government data might shift the odds in much of American life. You could study the vaccination data, for instance, and create heat maps for disease. "If you could randomly drop someone with measles somewhere in the United States, where would you have the biggest risk of an epidemic?" said DJ. "Where are epidemics waiting to happen? These questions, when you have access to data, you can do things. Everyone is focused on how data is a weapon. Actually, if we don't have data, we're screwed."

His memos were never read, DJ suspects. At any rate, he's never heard a peep about them. And he came to see there was nothing arbitrary or capricious about the Trump administration's attitude toward public data. Under each act of data suppression usually lay a narrow commercial motive: a gun lobbyist, a coal company, a poultry company. "The NOAA webpage used to have a link to weather forecasts," he said. "It was highly, highly popular. I saw it had been buried. And I asked: Now, why would they bury that?" Then he realized: the man Trump nominated to run NOAA thought that people who wanted a weather forecast should have to pay him for it. There was a rift in

American life that was now coursing through American government. It wasn't between Democrats and Republicans. It was between the people who were in it for the mission, and the people who were in it for the money.

━━━

The first time DJ Patil met Kathy Sullivan, he'd gone to talk to her about how she might better use data. He wound up learning from her how he might better approach his new mission. "She said something very insightful. She said working for the government, you need to imagine you are tied down, Gulliver-style. And if you want to even wiggle your big toe, first you need to ask permission. And that if you can imagine that and still imagine getting things done, you'll get things done."

The single most important source of data for the weather models are the satellites. The geostationary satellites hover over the equator, taking pictures of whatever is happening beneath them. The polar satellites circle the globe from North Pole to South Pole and gather data from the entire planet. They take soundings of the temperature and moisture in the atmosphere; measure vegetation coverage; monitor ozone levels; detect hot spots and so are able to report fires before people on the ground even know they have been lit; and feed weather forecasting models not just in the United States but in Europe and Asia. Without the information supplied by the polar satellites, weather forecasts everywhere would be worse. You'd be more likely to turn up at the airport and find that your flight had been canceled, or to be surprised by a wildfire, or to be hit without warning by a storm. "We ran the no-satellite experiment in Galveston in 1900," says Tim Schmit, a career NOAA researcher who has spent the last twenty-two years creating new and better satellite images of Earth. "Ten thousand people died."

Kathy Sullivan's life after her astronaut career had been one ambitious science project after another. She'd spent the first three years as NOAA's chief scientist. From there she'd gone on to run the Center of Science and Industry, a 320,000-square-foot museum and research center in Columbus, Ohio. After a decade of running that, she was hired in 2006 by Ohio State University to be the first director of their new science and math education center. When she returned to NOAA, in 2011, a polar satellite launched in the 1990s was approaching the end of its useful life. Its replacement was late, mired in political controversy, and facing cuts to a budget it had already exceeded. "She walks in the door and finds that the decisions made by a lot of other people are about to screw us all," said DJ Patil. "Now it's a question of national security. Because you won't be able to see the storms." A storm that went unseen, to DJ's way of thinking, belonged in the same category as a terrorist who went undetected.

The Clinton administration had asked three different agencies—the Department of Defense, NASA, and NOAA—to manage the polar satellites. The collaboration hadn't gone well. "The dynamic was a typical Washington sociopathic thing mixed up with a lack of leadership," said a former NOAA official. "Three agencies is hard. Because when you're busy or something annoys you, you can just assume or pretend that someone else will handle it. It's also hard because nobody wants to be responsible when things go badly. It's hard to control headlines and explain complicated things. Congress sends agencies very mixed signals, changes budgets, moves on to new things, speaks with many voices. Administrations and Congress don't often agree or even know about all the things the agencies are working on. Everybody blames someone else, and whoever is better at the blame game usually comes out on top. And the Department of Defense always comes out on top because it has the most resources and protective reflexes and friends."

The Obama administration had broken up the marriage between NASA and the Department of Defense and handed the entire mess to NOAA. But the NOAA to which Kathy Sullivan returned had drifted further in the direction it had been heading when she'd left. While the weather forecasts from inside it had gotten better and better, the political climate outside it had gotten worse and worse. Working at NOAA—or anyplace else in the federal government—could not be more different from working at NASA. When you were an astronaut, everyone loved you. When you told people that you worked for NASA they were usually curious, and even a bit informed. There was a reason for this, over and above the drama of the work: NASA had been encouraged, right from the start, to promote itself. "NASA was allowed to tell its story to the world," Kathy said. "There was a conscious need to publicize, because it was meant to restore confidence. NASA had heroes." NOAA didn't have heroes or drama. Or, rather, it had drama, and people who had done genuinely heroic things, but the American public never heard about any of it. It had people like Tim Schmit, the satellite guy, whose work had saved thousands of American lives. "NOAA has a hidden utility problem," said Kathy. "You cannot market NOAA. You *really* cannot market NOAA. Over the last several decades they not only don't get marketed. They are routinely slandered."

The relationship between the people and their government troubled her. The government was the mission of an entire society: why was the society undermining it? "I'm routinely appalled by how profoundly ignorant even highly educated people are when it comes to the structure and function of our government," she said. "The sense of identity as Citizen has been replaced by Consumer. The idea that government should serve the citizens like a waiter or concierge, rather than in a 'collective good' sense."

Her first big task upon returning to NOAA was to fix the polar satellite, and she did it. "She's unflappable with whiny politicians and lawyers," says a former NOAA official, who watched Sullivan attack the problem. "She was good at saying, 'Stop bothering my people and let them do their job.'" She got a new polar satellite, launched in November 2017, back on schedule, but with a twist: she arranged it so that the problems that had bedeviled her predecessors would not trouble her successors. "Of the many incredibly stupid things that a person can do on this planet, one is to build and buy a single satellite, when you know you'll need more of them," she said. There was no reason that NOAA could not budget for, and begin to plan, the next two, three, or four satellites; there were even economies of scale for some of the complicated parts. The problem was that no one in government liked to pay now if they could pay later. Nevertheless, she somehow persuaded the relevant parties in Congress and NOAA to make a deal for multiple satellites.

The ins and outs of how she'd done all this would have made for an excellent Harvard Business School case study—or a briefing memo for the new Trump administration. But that memo would never be read. The first Trump budget proposed removing the money in NOAA's budget that she'd secured for future satellites. The Trump people would never call her, but if they had she would have offered them one simple piece of advice. "You need to figure out what you want your leadership team to be intentional about—because if they aren't intentional about it, it won't happen. There's hundreds of things that will naturally happen. And then there are the things that won't." One of the things that wouldn't happen is satellites getting built on time, within budget. Another was that Americans would die, if you didn't work hard to figure out what was going on inside their heads.

That had been her next big project. A Weather-Ready Nation, she called it. The Joplin tornado had been the catalyst. It had various ambitions—making communities more responsive to the weather, making fishing stocks more resilient to the climate—but at its heart was the desire to better prepare Americans to face threats. Kathy had helped to install Louis Uccellini as head of the National Weather Service; he shared her passion for the problem. The meteorologists inside the Weather Service were bothered that people didn't respond as expected to their warnings. But then they were weather geeks. Scientists. "I can't trace exactly where or when or how the realization dawned [on us] that the jargon-laden bulletins were not comprehensible to users," said Kathy. "Or that people didn't respond to raw data; they respond to other human beings, trusted voices. Or that the punch line—what this storm may do to you—was often buried after many paragraphs of geeky weather details. Or that normal humans don't understand probabilities and cannot translate a wind speed or rain rate into tangible worries about the roof coming off or being knee-deep in water. You don't particularly care what the wind speed at five hundred millibars is. You want to know: What's it going to do to my house?"

So they set out to understand the people on the receiving end of the forecasts. It wasn't enough to farm the problem out to others. They needed people in NOAA studying the way Americans responded to warnings, and to risk. NOAA was an agency staffed by hard scientists facing a problem that cried out for psychologists and behavioral economists. "The odd group, whatever the odd group is, needs to be in the room," she said. "There's all sorts of inclinations *not* to do that. The existing powers say,

'Leave me alone, and let me do what I want to do.'" She wanted to start a conversation inside the agency, with the understanding that they couldn't predict exactly where it might lead.

It reminded her of something that had happened just after the *Challenger* explosion. American cities were planning to name streets and schools for the astronauts, but that had felt inadequate to her—and to the astronauts' spouses. Everyone who'd been close to the astronauts wanted the meaning of their lives to be better understood through their deaths. "They all had this shared joy of bringing science and technology education to lots of people," said Kathy. "We asked, how do we continue that?"

By the end of 1986, the astronauts' families had decided to create a science education program—though of what sort they did not yet know. The spouses asked Kathy to figure it out. She started by bringing them all together, to explain how uncomfortable it was going to be to create an entirely new thing when they didn't know exactly what it would be. They'd need to invite many odd groups into the room and give them the power to influence the project. "I told them, 'It's your legacy to the crew. But to do it you need to create a network of people who feel they can shape it. The conversation really matters. Converse means exchange with. It does not mean transmit at. That's how you get new thinking.'" She'd heard a line once that still resonated with her: *The only thing any of us can do completely on our own is to have the start of a good idea.*

She found all sorts of odd groups, outsiders to the space

project, unknown to the astronauts' families, who might be relevant to the new mission: teachers, museum professionals, curriculum supervisors, textbook publishers, exhibition designers, video-tech types, and so on. Plus, an architect. She gathered all these people in Biosphere 2, in Oracle, Arizona, "to get everyone out of their ruts." Pretty quickly the architect turned the event into a presentation of his plan for the building. Kathy and the others could see that he hadn't listened to a word anyone had said. She let him go the next day. In the end, the group discussion led to a course aimed at middle-school students. There are now fifty-two Challenger Centers around the world, and they have taught four and a half million students.

In the aftermath of the Joplin tornado, the odd group—the new kids in school—were the psychologists and behavioral economists. In 2014 Kathy helped to persuade Congress to write into law the idea that social science was part of NOAA's mission. The agency could now hire people to collect a different kind of data—data that would enable them to figure out what exactly was going on inside the minds of the American people, so that it might save their lives.

═══════

The funny thing about tornadoes is that no one knows how powerful they are until they've hit something. The National Weather Service can tell you days in advance what to make of a hurricane—the strength of its winds, and the size of its storm surge, along with the likelihood of its hitting your city instead of someone else's. As you sit on your porch in New Orleans deciding whether you should get in your car and drive to Memphis to avoid a hurricane, you have a pretty good idea what you are in for if you don't. Tornadoes aren't like that. Like the rest of the weather in the continental United States, they move from west to east, but the paths they take are random. Their force can be judged only after the fact, by the damage they've done. If a hurricane is another night in a bad marriage, a tornado is a blind date.

The scale for judging tornadoes, after the fact, runs from 0 to 5. It's called the Fujita scale. What makes it different from most scales is that it is consistently terrifying from beginning to end. An F1 tornado merely peels roof surfaces off houses and knocks cars off the road. By F2, mobile homes are being destroyed and cows are flying through the air.

Kim Klockow was seven years old, playing in a field in Naperville, Illinois, when she caught sight of her first tornado. She didn't know what she was seeing. "I saw the booby clouds," she recalled—the breast-shaped mammatus clouds that accompany big storms. "I was looking at the anvil of the storm." No one ever actually saw the tornado until it wiped out some of Plainfield, Illinois, on August 28, 1990. It had eluded radar and, wrapped in a rainstorm, had been invisible to the naked eye. The National Weather Service didn't even issue a warning until an hour after the event. Afterward it would go down as the only F5 tornado ever recorded in the Chicago suburbs. In an F5, cars become missiles and big, well-constructed houses simply vanish. Kim's parents had driven her through Plainfield two days later, and she'd seen buildings she'd been inside of reduced to rubble or entirely gone, like in *The Wizard of Oz*. "You don't think of buildings as being dangerous," she said. "You think of buildings as being a place you were safe."

That tornado had killed twenty-nine people, injured hundreds more, and traumatized the region. The following year, as another storm approached, people were on edge. When the wind kicked up and the hail began to ricochet off the pavement, Kim was in the neighboring city of Joliet, with her mother and two-year-old sister, registering for French lessons. Her mother grabbed them and fled. As they sped toward home, Kim could see her mother watching behind them. "We were actually being chased by the storm," she recalled. "The hail sounded like bullets hitting the car." For some reason her mother insisted that the windows remain down: hail fell onto Kim's lap. "My mother was saying the same thing over and over, but I didn't know what it was. She was saying Hail Marys." They peeled into the driveway and her mother screamed at her, "Get into the house, and get downstairs!" She'd run and hid—and came away with the feeling that it was only by luck that her house had not been blown away. "After that," said Kim, "any weather information we got, I wanted to know. This is actually the story of every meteorologist. We are a whole field of people who are child trauma cases."

One hot May morning I picked Kim Klockow up from

her office at the NWS Storm Prediction Center, in the National Weather Center Building, in Norman, Oklahoma. The center is a joint venture between the University of Oklahoma and NOAA, and about as perfectly situated as an institution can be. The south-central United States is the planet's convective sweet spot: here the warm air from the Gulf of Mexico collides with the cool air tumbling down over the Rocky Mountains and creates storms with more energy than nuclear bombs. Texas has twice as many tornadoes as Oklahoma, but Oklahoma has them in about a fourth the space. Kansas has about a third more tornadoes each year than Oklahoma, but Kansas is a third again bigger than Oklahoma and has a third fewer people. If you have some need or desire to witness dramatic collisions between people and weather, Oklahoma is your place. "Being here during a serious tornado event is better than football," says Hank Jenkins-Smith, who runs the University of Oklahoma's National Institute for Risk and Resilience—which is as aptly sited as the Storm Prediction Center. At the top of the National Weather Center Building is a skybox, facing west, and equipped with special blast-proof glass, to watch the approaching tornadoes.

Kim came to the University of Oklahoma in 2006 as a graduate student to study . . . well, she hadn't been sure what she was going to study. She'd received her undergraduate degree in both meteorology and economics and, up to that point, focused on the economic impact of storms. What happens to the finances of a community hit by a tornado, for instance. The work interested her, but she also felt something was missing. "I just felt that classical economics wasn't really hitting on the questions that meteorologists were asking," she said.

Her frustration led her first into behavioral economics, which was no more than psychology made respectable to the sort of people who tended to think psychology was all bullshit. She set out to investigate a problem: How do people respond to risk? How might you influence that response, to their benefit? If you told someone that a tornado might be headed his way in a week, he'd give you a funny look and go about his business. If you pointed out to that same person the tornado bearing down on his house, he'd dive for cover. She wanted to figure out when and why complacency turned to alarm and when and why alarm turned into action.

In December 2010 she was finishing up her thesis when an adviser suggested that what she really needed to do was some fieldwork. Go out and interview real-live Americans who had responded to the news that their lives might be at risk. "They said, 'If anything happens in 2011, we want you to do a case study,'" said Kim. "Then Joplin happens."

For complicated reasons, she set out to survey people not in Joplin but in Alabama and Mississippi. A few weeks before the catastrophe in Missouri, tornadoes had wreaked havoc in those states, despite excellent warnings from the National Weather Service. What became known as the 2011 Super Outbreak spawned 360 tornadoes that killed 324 and injured thousands more.

In its wake a pair of ideas sprang up and gained traction—

both inside and outside the Weather Service. The first was that the twenty-minute warnings that had been issued had not given people enough time to escape. Powerful congressmen from tornado-prone states insisted that the National Weather Service needed to improve its ability to predict tornadoes to the point where they could warn people an hour in advance. And the National Weather Service had simply nodded and accepted the challenge. "Everyone in the Weather Service is so drawn to the mission of helping other people," said Kim. "That's what was so crushing about 2011. *Oh, I may have just spent my entire career possibly doing nothing.*"

But Kim wondered about the wisdom of their new ambition. "It's hard to talk to dead people about the decisions they made," she said. "It's one of the challenges we have. But I was trying to ask what they would do if they'd had more time." She interviewed survivors in Alabama and Mississippi and came away with a startling insight: time might be beside the point. It wasn't that people who had apparently ignored the government's alerts had been oblivious to them. "They were *all* aware of the warnings," she said. "It isn't that people wantonly disregard warnings. It's that they think it won't hit *them*." The paper Kim subsequently coauthored pointed out that people associate "home" with "safety." This feeling was reinforced each and every day that nothing horrible happened inside of it. People acquired a "false confidence that they would not be hit." Some inner calculation led them to believe that, if it's never happened here, it never will.

The people who had failed to seek shelter in the way that, say, a meteorologist thinks they should have done had one thing in common: they lived in homes that had never been struck by a tornado. They inhabited a region prone to tornadoes; they had lived through many tornado warnings; but right up until 2011 they themselves had been spared a direct hit. They offered Kim lots of explanations for their immunity to catastrophic risk. They claimed that tornadoes never crossed the river they lived on, for instance. Or that tornadoes always split as they approached their town. Or that tornadoes always followed the highway. Or that tornadoes never struck the old Indian burial grounds. People who lived on the west side of a big city felt more exposed than people on the east side: they believed buildings offered protection. A lot of people seemed to believe that hills did, too. "Where tornadoes go is totally random," Kim said. "The steering winds are in the upper atmosphere. But people are not thinking of the forces of the atmosphere. They are thinking of their place on the ground." Psychologists have long known that people see patterns where none exist. Londoners during the Blitz felt they'd deduced the targets of German bombers by where the bombs had fallen, when the bombs had been dropped randomly over the city. Americans routinely made the same mistake with the weather.

Soon we were driving west together, Kim Klockow and I. A few minutes after leaving the Storm Prediction Center, we passed from Norman into Moore, and from one wan row of shopping malls and car dealerships to another. Here was another curious example of man's attitude toward the things that might kill him—and another illustration of Kim's point. The people in Norman think that tornadoes don't hit them; the people in Moore believe they are especially prone to being hit by tornadoes. Moore's sense of doom dates back to May 3, 1999, when a tornado crossed the freeway and cut through the town. It was a mile wide and generated wind speeds of 302 miles per hour, the highest ever recorded on earth. It killed thirty-six people, including a woman who had sheltered exactly as experts had instructed, by lying in a bathtub and covering herself with a mattress. (A car crashed through her roof and landed on her.)

On May 20, 2013, another F5 tornado struck Moore and killed twenty-four people, including seven children in a school, after an interior wall collapsed on them. Between those two events, Moore had been hit by two F4 tornadoes and been dealt glancing blows by several small ones. By 2013 its reputation as a magnet for tornadoes was sealed. "The perception of risk of the people in Moore is about twice that of people living in Norman," said Kim. Moore is the only town in Oklahoma to have adopted building codes to defend itself against the wind; it has even devised a scheme that allows worried parents to bus their children to schools that have storm shelters. "The people in Norman are less likely to start preparing during a tornado watch than the people in Moore," said Kim. "The people in Norman think that Moore is more likely to be hit than

Norman. And this might be the most educated population, about tornado risk, in the world. *Hundreds* of meteorologists live in Norman."

The road to the weather of the future is straight and hot. It leads after an hour or so to the city of El Reno. "You can still see this one," said Kim. "In the trees." Eleven days after the 2013 Moore tornado, there had been another spin-up, right here. Within minutes, what became known as the El Reno tornado was 2.6 miles wide, the widest tornado ever seen, and headed for Oklahoma City. "Tornadoes leave scars that are visible from space, when they are big enough," Kim says.

The second idea that gained traction after the 2011 tornadoes was that people simply failed to appreciate what happened when a tornado hit a mobile home, or a car, or really anything that wasn't bolted to the ground. If the warnings highlighted the potential destruction, the thinking went, people might pay them more attention. "Impact based warnings," the new warnings were called, though the differences between them and the old warnings were fairly subtle. The Weather Service did not generally communicate directly with the public. It issued warnings to local emergency managers and the TV meteorologists, who then passed on what they'd been told. But the Weather Service now encouraged the weather media to help people to imagine what might happen if they did not seek shelter. "The idea was the people just don't know how bad it is," said Kim. "If they knew how bad it is, they'd take action."

COMPLETE DESTRUCTION OF ENTIRE NEIGHBORHOODS
IS LIKELY. MANY WELL–BUILT HOMES AND BUSINESSES
WILL BE COMPLETELY SWEPT FROM THEIR FOUNDATION.
DEBRIS WILL BLOCK MOST ROADWAYS. MASS DEVASTA-
TION IS HIGHLY LIKELY, MAKING THE AREA UNRECOG-
NIZABLE TO SURVIVORS.

And so on.

The market for weather news in Oklahoma is fiercely competitive. The local TV weather anchors already felt pressure to make the reality more interesting than it was. "They glom onto the worst-case scenario days before we can have any confidence," says Kim. "A government agency does not have an incentive to hype. Private companies have an incentive to hype. The problem when you hype is that you reduce confidence in *all* weather forecasts, because no one knows the source of the information." About thirty minutes before the El Reno tornado reached Oklahoma City, a TV weatherman named Mike Morgan told his viewers that anyone who wasn't underground was doomed. Most people had no underground place to go. The soil in Oklahoma is a sandy clay floating on a high water table: the place on the planet where people most desperately need to dig a hole to hide happens also to be a place in which it is expensive to dig. Though a car might be the single worst place to be in a tornado, tens of thousands of Oklahomans fled by car. Instantly the southbound lanes of the interstate became a parking lot. The El Reno tornado bore down on what amounted to a miles-long traffic jam. . . .

And then it lifted. By sheer luck the El Reno tornado killed only eight people—most of whom had been fleeing it. What didn't happen did not get nearly as much attention as it deserved, in Kim's view. "If it hadn't lifted, if it had continued on its path, the estimate of the fatalities would have been Katrina-level. It's the worst catastrophe that almost happened. In the most tornado-savvy population in the world. It was really jarring."

El Reno had been her turning point. "It struck me: How could we think we could help people without understanding people?" she said. "The way we have approached things is by learning about the threat. We've ignored the people being threatened." She thought that impact based warnings were intellectually dishonest: How could you warn about the impact of a storm whose force you would only be able to discern after the fact? She was also pretty sure that people knew what a tornado could do to them. The people in Alabama and Mississippi knew. So did the people in Joplin. Their problem, as she saw it, was a different sort of failure of the imagination. People could not imagine that all those tornadoes that had wound up hitting other people could instead have hit *them*. The sirens had become fake news. The government needed to find ways to make the news feel real.

A few months later, she moved to Washington, DC, on a congressional fellowship and went to work for a senator who sat on the committee that oversaw the Commerce Department. "I'm gunning for something inside NOAA," she said. "You have to have people on the inside to make the change." In late 2014 her ambition collided with Kathy Sullivan's, and NOAA hired Kim Klockow to be its first, and only, social scientist. She became the odd group in the room.

She'd spent three years in the job. She'd hoped to create a social science unit on the top of the agency that could both direct a research program and spread what it learned through the Weather Service. "The problem with our science is that it is new," she said. "And we don't know how to make people not die. We need data on what led a person to do what they did. We need observations of humans responding to weather information." She'd made some progress. She'd also been frustrated. "Barry Myers [AccuWeather's CEO] turned up at a meeting and said that I shouldn't be doing what I was doing," she said. "Because it's marketing. But it's not marketing. It's saving lives. The question became: What can we do in this space without interfering with the profits of AccuWeather?"

And then Trump was elected. She'd planned to return to Oklahoma anyway, but now she did it with a sense that she might be better off starting small, rather than trying to change the entire Weather Service from the top. "The inspiration came from Dr. Sullivan—she advised me to rely on 'small bets' to make significant organizational change, not to try to force big, sudden change from the top."

It was May 2017, and Kim Klockow had been back in an office at the University of Oklahoma only a few weeks when the meteorologists in the Storm Prediction Center forecast a storm in the Texas Panhandle. She hopped into a car with another meteorologist and went west, to where the weather came from. "When I was in DC I lost my sense of direction," she said. "In DC this is not material knowledge." She'd found the storm in Texas, and then turned around and followed it from behind into Oklahoma. The little girl once terrified by the storm that was chasing her was now a woman chasing a storm. In Oklahoma, as often happened, the storm met an atmosphere more favorable to it, and it grew. "I saw it," she said. "It was a beast." She'd arrived just outside of Elk City when she heard the Weather Service issue its tornado warning— and so she'd stopped. "You don't chase into a city," she said. "You don't chase to see death and destruction."

At length, she and I drive the hot, flat road past the Cherokee Trading Post & Boot Outlet and arrive in Elk City. Elk City is where we'd been heading all along.

———

Lonnie Risenhoover had been managing emergencies in Beckham County in one way or another for forty years. Before he became emergency manager for the entire county, he'd worked as a fireman in Elk City, where he was born and raised. His great-grandfather had moved there in the late nineteenth century, before Oklahoma was even a state, and the family had remained ever since. There were only about twenty-five thousand people in the whole of Beckham County, about half of those in Elk City, and Lonnie knew most of them. He'd seen all the storms, too, but the county had been lucky that way. "Most of the tornadoes are real rural," he said. " 'Well, we had a tornado and Joe's chicken coop just blowed away.' " *Tornayda.* The one thing the storms had in common was the hysteria about them generated by the TV news stations in Oklahoma City. "If there's an icicle hanging off the corner of the house it's 'hey, there's an icicle hangin' off the corner of the house, we're gonna go live with it!' " *A-sicle.*

The information Lonnie took seriously came directly from the National Weather Service. ("If the Weather Service had a TV channel, everyone would just watch that.") Every morning he woke up and checked NWSChat— the Weather Service's tool for communicating with local emergency managers. The morning of May 16, 2017, had a slightly different feel to it than usual, though Lonnie didn't immediately put his finger on why. They said a storm was coming from the Panhandle, but storms were always coming from the Panhandle. There was no tornado warning.

But a tornado wasn't like a winter storm. The models hadn't gotten to the point where they could predict a tornado before it happened, in the way they could bigger weather systems. The Weather Service could only issue a tornado warning after it had *seen* the tornado, either with its radar or one of its spotters. "What I noticed," said Lonnie, "was that they'd changed some of the language they used. They said 'tornado emergency.' It used to be just a 'tornado warning.' "

He left the chat more worried than usual. The storm might be a problem, he thought.

The Elk City Fire Department had a few tornado spotters, but they just sat at fixed points: the city had blind spots. "The western part of Beckham County, we didn't have many storm spotters," Lonnie said. "And I'm basically a one-man shop. So I can do everything I need to do in my vehicle." His truck had so much gear in it that you didn't want to ask what it all was, for fear that the explanations would never end. From his truck he could measure the wind speed, see the radar, and stay in touch with the Weather Service, even if his phone lost service. He got into his truck and drove west, to find a place from which he could see as much of the earth's surface as possible.

If you were just passing through you'd think Beckham County was essentially flat. Brownish-yellow wheat fields and pastureland as far as the eye can see. In his forty years of storm spotting, Lonnie had come to know every slight undulation in the terrain. In twenty minutes he was parked on some of the highest ground in the county, facing southwest. When the meteorologists from the Storm Prediction Center go out to chase storms, they chase them from behind, to make sure they aren't overtaken by the tornado. Lonnie just sat there, waiting for the tornado to come at him. "My wife used to go with me," he said. "Now she won't. She says, 'You scare me.'"

Then he saw it. Or maybe he didn't. "I seen a funnel," he said. "But I wasn't going to start calling it a tornado until I start seeing grass or something else it's picking up." Whatever he was seeing vanished after maybe a minute. He couldn't tell how fast it might be moving toward him, or how far away it was. He didn't want to trigger a warning unnecessarily—if he did that, people might not believe the next one. At the same time, what he was hearing just then from the National Weather Service was not normal. They hadn't seen the tornado, but they were acting almost as if they had. "I kept getting information," he said. "They were feeding me a lot of information. And I thought, This is really, really going to be bad."

He was utterly exposed. Alone, out in a massive storm that might, or might not, be concealing a tornado. He wheeled his truck around and hauled ass. Instead of heading straight back toward Elk City, he drove south, along the width of the storm. As he drove, he reported what he was seeing to the Weather Service, and the Weather Service was reporting what it knew to him. The anemometer on top of his truck recorded the speed of the winds being sucked *into* the storm: 79 miles per hour. The Weather Service told him they'd had reports of hail that was bigger than baseballs. Traveling 80 miles an hour down a dirt road in a pelting rain, he was all the time thinking about what to do: Wait, to make sure he'd seen what he'd seen? Or phone the Weather Service and trigger a tornado warning that set off the town siren? "So you sit here and make this decision," he said. "And I think: Who is going to dispute my word? So I called the Weather Service."

He came upon a sight that pulled him up short: downed power lines. The poles that had held them were gone. As if they had never been there. The tornado had crossed his path and leaped ahead of him: how he did not know. He'd thought the storm was chasing him; now, apparently, he was chasing the storm. Then he saw it, but it took him a moment to realize what he was seeing. It wasn't like a tornado in the movies. "It looks like the cloud was on the ground," he said. "It was a thousand yards wide."

For the next twenty minutes he followed the cloud's trail of destruction. Dead cows everywhere. Shattered oak trees. A school bus turned into a twisted pile of metal. Cars piled on top of each other, upside down, in a pond. He knew the landscape well enough to see what it was missing: big trees, telephone poles, mobile homes. "You could say, 'There used to be a house there,'" he said. One house he passed was only partially destroyed. It looked as if some giant had tried to dissect it: the front half had been ripped away so that he could see all the way back into the television room. The big red barn that had been right next to it had vanished without a trace. The house belonged to Miss Finley, an old woman who lived alone. Lonnie's job wasn't emergency rescue—he was meant to be the eyes on the storm—but he stopped anyway, to see if he could find her. As he searched the ruins, a truck came flying up. "It was Miss Finley's son," said Lonnie. "He said she had gone to the town shelter."

When you are chasing a cloud, there's a question of how fast to go. Lonnie perhaps went too fast. Soon he found himself staring at a subdivision of new homes, all destroyed. "I'm looking over at these houses, and all I see is sticks," he said. Debris was now crashing around his truck. He looked up and saw a huge piece of tin. "I got large stuff falling out the sky," he said. "I can't go any further."

All along, his phone had been ringing. The Weather Channel. CNN. MSNBC. All these TV people were calling to find out what had happened. The truth is, he didn't know, and it took him a bit of time to figure it out. It turned out that more than two hundred homes in Elk City had been destroyed, along with thirty-eight businesses. A lot of property had been lost. But—and here's what shocked him—people had mostly kept out of harm's way. Karen Snyder had refused to leave her cats and had been found, alive and well, with the ruins of her house on top of her. Gene Mikles had called the sheriff to ask if he should seek shelter, had been told that he should, and had started to the shelter but then returned to his home to grab his phone. He'd been found dead on the ground outside. "Only one fatality and eight bruises," said Lonnie. "What I think happened is that people listened to the warning." The town shelter had been so crowded that they'd had to lead people into the basement of the fire station.

On the morning of May 16, 2017, purely by chance, a team of researchers in the Storm Prediction Center had been testing a new tornado model. Even after they varied their assumptions about the conditions of the atmosphere, the model generated tornadoes. The images were clear and consistent: later the researchers said it was as if they had seen the storm in the real world. Everyone in the weather business believed this was the future: the ability to predict a tornado, in theory, before it spun up. The ability to imagine it, with precision, before you could see it. Now it was happening. The researchers informed the

Weather Service meteorologist on duty, and the meteorologist issued a different kind of alert. Not a warning, but a warning that a warning was very likely coming; and it had prodded Lonnie to behave as he might not have done. It made him feel the threat was real—that the storm might hit *him*. That feeling had caused him to trigger a warning a few minutes earlier than he might otherwise have done. "The main thing I was so excited about is we were able to set off the sirens thirty minutes before it hit," he said.

Lonnie Risenhoover knew nothing about what had happened inside the Storm Prediction Center. "That was a prototype," he said. "It was the first time they'd used it. I didn't know it." But he knew what he was hearing from the Weather Service staff sounded different from what he usually heard. They'd given him, in effect, a clearer sense of the odds. They'd done what Kim Klockow had been advocating for: don't tell people what the tornado will do to them if it hits them. Instead, persuade them that the threat is real. "People in Oklahoma, they're going to credit the media," said Lonnie. "Because that's where they are getting their information. But who they should credit is the Weather Service. The Weather Service—they don't give themselves enough credit. They say, 'We're just doing a job.' But I don't know where we'd be without them."

At dinner one night I played a game with Kim Klockow and her friends Hank Jenkins-Smith and Carol Silva, the co-directors of the University of Oklahoma's Center for Risk & Crisis Management. They'd devoted their lives to studying people's response to risk. I'd wondered who, and

THE FIFTH RISK

what, was most likely to survive a tornado. If you were a tree, for instance, you'd much rather be a willow than an oak, as a willow tree bends. The risk experts all agreed they'd bet money on a horse over a cow, and on a dog over a cat. ("Dogs are more likely to obey.") They became less certain when we turned to the more complicated matter of human beings. Because they were intellectually honest academics, they were reluctant to generalize. "People aren't necessarily good at managing one kind of risk just because they are good at managing another kind of risk," said Carol. "People will be deathly afraid of one kind of risk and blasé about another."

Still, they played along, in a hypothetical game of survival. They all agreed that you'd obviously bet money on a rich person over a poor person. ("People who live in mobile homes are thirty times more likely to die.") They'd take a parent over a pet owner, as animals aren't allowed in public storm shelters. ("Pets will kill you.") They argued a bit, but finally decided they'd take a woman over a man, as men tended to be more risk-seeking. "Men go outside and look around," said Carol. "You see this in the tornado videos on YouTube. The wife sticking her head out the door screaming at her husband, 'Hey, git your ass inside!'" Finally, I asked: a liberal or a conservative? Eighty-three and a half percent of Beckham County had voted for Donald Trump. What did that say about their ability to survive a tornado? The liberal has the advantage of trusting the government's warning, said Hank, but the conservative has advantages, too. It depended on what kind of conservative he was, they decided. If he was a radical individualist, he was a bad risk: you'd bet on the liberal to survive. But if the conservative belonged to a strong social network—a church, say—he might hear a tornado warning, and trust it, before it was too late. "What you need is one person inside the network who is a trusted source, who trusts the government," said Hank. You need Lonnie Risenhoover.

I had in mind a final game of survivor, but I never got around to asking them about it. Who is more likely to survive a tornado: the person who has personally experienced one, or the person who has not, and *why*? The advantage of experience is more or less obvious; the disadvantage of not having had the experience less so. But it might be the more important factor. All kinds of things might happen to you in life. By sheer accident only a few of them do. That tiny subset shapes your view of the world, to an alarming degree. If a tornado has never hit your town, you think it never will. You might try to imagine what will befall you if it does. The reality of the thing will still shock you.

In the weeks after the Elk City tornado, Lonnie Risenhoover toured the damage with various government officials. A man from the Federal Emergency Management Agency came through to determine who was eligible for disaster relief. While driving the man around Elk City, Lonnie spotted Miss Finley. Her house was a ruin and her barn was gone: surely she was eligible for relief. Lonnie stopped so the FEMA guy might speak with her. "You know," said Miss Finley, "for the last ten years I prayed for a tornado to come and take that barn. I didn't think it would take the house, too." She seemed to think her reasoning self-evident. The FEMA guy said he didn't understand: Why had she been praying for a tornado to take her barn? "Every time I pull out of the driveway I'm looking at that red barn," she said. "And every time I pull into the driveway I'm looking at the red barn." At which point Lonnie asked the FEMA guy if he was ready to leave. He wasn't. He was still puzzled: Why did it bother the woman to look at her red barn? "That barn," said Miss Finley, "is where my husband committed suicide ten years ago."

And so you might have good reason to pray for a tornado, whether it comes in the shape of swirling winds, or a politician. You imagine the thing doing the damage that you would like to see done, and no more. It's what you fail to imagine that kills you.

ACKNOWLEDGMENTS

I'd like to thank Graydon Carter for a fabulous decade-long run at *Vanity Fair* that ended with the second chapter of this book. It was never obvious that anyone would want to read what had interested me about the United States government. Doug Stumpf, my magazine editor for the past decade, persuaded me that, at this strange moment in American history, others might share my enthusiasm. As the material mushroomed into a book and threatened to receive more attention than I expected, I was relieved and grateful that Janet Byrne agreed once again to make me appear to be a better writer than I am. And I'm not sure what I would do without Starling Lawrence, who has edited my books since I began writing them. Podcasts?